:N TOWARD MADNESS

New Approaches to Midwestern Studies

SERIES EDITORS: PAUL FINKELMAN AND L. DIANE BARNES

DRIVEN TOWARD MADNESS

The Fugitive Slave Margaret Garner and Tragedy on the Ohio

Nikki M. Taylor

OHIO UNIVERSITY PRESS — ATHENS

Ohio University Press, Athens, Ohio 45701
ohioswallow.com
© 2016 by Ohio University Press

To obtain permission to quote, reprint, or otherwise reproduce or distribute material from Ohio University Press publications, please contact our rights and permis-
sions department at (740) 593-1154 or (740) 593-4536 (fax).

Printed in the United States of America
Ohio University Press books are printed on acid-free paper ⊗ ™
Cover credit: Thomas Satterwhite Noble, *The Modern Medea* (1867).
From the Collection of the National Underground Railroad Freedom Center.

27 26 25 24 23 22 21 20 19 18 17 16   5 4 3 2 1

Library of Congress Cataloging-in-Publication Data
Names: Taylor, Nikki Marie, 1972– author.
Title: Driven toward madness : the fugitive slave Margaret Garner and tragedy
on the Ohio / Nikki M. Taylor.
Description: Athens : Ohio University Press, 2016. | Series: New approaches
to midwestern studies | Includes bibliographical references and index.
Identifiers: LCCN 2016041893| ISBN 9780821421598 (hc : alk. paper) | ISBN
9780821421604 (pb : alk. paper) | ISBN 9780821445860 (pdf)
Subjects: LCSH: Garner, Margaret, 1834–1858. | Fugitive
slaves—Kentucky—Biography. | Fugitive slaves—Legal status, laws,
etc.—United States. | Fugitive slaves—Legal status, laws,
etc.—Ohio—Cincinnati. | Garner, Margaret, 1834–1858—Trials, litigation,
etc. | Infanticide—Ohio—Cincinnati—Case studies.
Classification: LCC E450.G225 T39 2016 | DDC 306.3/62092 [B] —dc23
LC record available at https://lccn.loc.gov/2016041893

For Black Women

and Their Unconquerable Spirits,

Past and Present

CONTENTS

ILLUSTRATIONS

SERIES EDITORS' PREFACE

For much of American history the term "Midwest" evoked images of endless fields of grain, flat, treeless landscapes, and homogenized populations in small towns. Most Americans hear "Midwest" and think of corn, wheat, soybeans, massive feedlots, huge pig farms, and countless dairy herds. The cinematic Midwest was River City, Iowa, in *The Music Man*; Dorothy trying to escape Oz and get back to Kansas; the iconic power of small-town basketball portrayed in *Hoosiers*; or a mythical baseball diamond in rural Iowa in *Field of Dreams*. In the late twentieth century, images of deindustrialization and decay linked the region to a new identity as the nation's Rust Belt. For too many Americans, the Midwest has been "flyover country."

This book series explores regional identity in the nation's past through the lens of the American Midwest. Stereotypical images of the region ignore the complexity and vibrancy of the region, as well as the vital role it has played—and continues to play—in the nation's economy, politics, and social history. In the antebellum and Civil War periods the Midwest was home to virulent racist opponents of black rights and black migration but also to a vibrant antislavery movement, the vigorous and often successful Underground Railroad, and the political and military leadership that brought an end to slavery and reframed the Constitution to provide at least formal racial equality. A midwestern president issued the Emancipation Proclamation, and midwestern generals led the armies that defeated the southern slaveocracy. Midwestern politicians authored the Thirteenth Amendment ending slavery and the Fourteenth Amendment mandating legal equality for all Americans. The political impact of the region is exemplified by the fact that from 1860 to 1932 only two elected presidents (Grover Cleveland and Woodrow Wilson) were not from the Midwest. Significantly, from 1864 until the 1930s every Chief Justice but one was also a midwesterner.

Much of the history of the Midwest has been about race. The political or cultural Midwest began with the passage of the Northwest Ordinance in 1787, which provided for a system of government and land distribution for the territories north and west of the Ohio River—present-day Ohio, Indiana, Illinois, Michigan, Wisconsin, and part of Minnesota. The Ordinance established the process of turning territories into states, but it is most remembered for Article VI, added at the last minute, banning slavery in the Northwest Territory. The antislavery article of the Ordinance was less effective than its authors anticipated. Perhaps a thousand or so slaves already lived in the Territory, mostly in what is today southern Indiana or southern Illinois. Thanks to proslavery interpretations of the Ordinance and stubborn persistence by the slave owners in the Territory, most of these people were held in bondage until the early nineteenth century, and some remained in servitude until the 1840s.

Even when they were no longer in bondage, African Americans endured discriminatory laws that made their settlement in the region difficult. In Ohio there was never any slavery or long-term indentured servitude, as there was in Indiana and Illinois. But blacks in the Buckeye State could not vote, serve on juries, or before 1849 even expect to attend a public school. Yet, despite this discrimination, free blacks and fugitive slaves poured into Ohio from the moment of statehood in 1803 until the Civil War. In 1803 there were fewer than 500 blacks in the state. By 1810 there were more than 2,000, and by 1830 the population was almost 10,000. The federal census found more than 25,000 African Americans in 1850 and more than 36,000 on the eve of the Civil War. The real number was certainly larger, because fugitive slaves entering the state did their best not be counted or even noticed by government officials.

By 1850 Ohio also had a strong and vibrant antislavery community. Opponents of slavery, like Joshua R. Giddings, Benjamin F. Wade, James Ashley, John Bingham, and most important of all, Salmon P. Chase, held state offices and represented the state in the House of Representatives and the Senate. Antislavery lawyers fought to protect fugitive slaves, and some whites pushed for increasing black rights. Racism was still common, and blacks suffered discrimination in many ways, but at the same time, one of the few integrated colleges in the country was in Oberlin, and at least one African American, John Mercer Langston, was elected to public office, even though blacks were prohibited from voting.

The Ohio River marked the boundary between slavery and freedom for thousands of African Americans who crossed the river to escape bondage. Many successfully made the transition from southern slavery to northern liberty, even if they did not have full equality. Ohio was a beacon for slaves who wanted to own themselves.

Nikki M. Taylor tells the story of a family of Kentucky slaves who saw Ohio as just such a beacon of freedom. The family managed to escape across the Ohio River, only to be captured in Cincinnati. What happened next was a tragic moment in American history. Rather than let her children be returned to bondage, their mother, Margaret Garner, attacked her offspring, managing to kill one of her children before being stopped. The incident incited sectional controversy. Southerners argued that only a crazy woman would kill her own children. Some northerners agreed, but others realized that the evils of slavery might drive a mother to do what was unspeakable: murder her own child. Was Margaret Garner insane or evil? Or was she rational in thinking that death was better than bondage? Had slavery driven her to madness, or was she reacting logically to the events of the moment, in a small house in Cincinnati, as slave catchers and law enforcement officials from Ohio tried to capture her and her family? This is the story that Nikki Taylor offers us.

Paul Finkelman
L. Diane Barnes

ACKNOWLEDGMENTS

My life would have little meaning without my spiritual grounding. I thank God for every ounce of support and inner strength that enabled me to finish this—my third—monograph. I also thank Ohio University Press, its board and editorial staff, for this opportunity. I am especially grateful to Director Gillian Berchowitz, as well as Diane Barnes and Paul Finkelman, for being a better publishing team than I could ever have dreamed of. I have nothing but the highest praise for the attention and time they have given to this book—as well as my first one, *Frontiers of Freedom*. Other presses might not have given either of these projects a chance, but this team believed in me, my vision, and capability. Perhaps that is what allowed them to put up with my countless delays. Gill Berchowitz is—hands-down—one of the most capable, intelligent, supportive, and nurturing editors in the game. I count it as an added bonus to have one of the leading legal scholars in Paul on my team. He responded to *every* one of my hysterical calls and emails at all hours asking for assistance detangling the legal issues in the case. He and Diane read more drafts of this manuscript than should be legal. I truly feel that this was a collective project.

I also acknowledge those who eagerly and graciously assisted me in this project. They include Ruth Wade Cox Brunings for early conversations about her perspective on this case. Although I may not agree with her, her insight helped me understand Kentucky culture, race relations, history, and memory. She very generously and graciously shared her research and allowed me to pick her brain about this case. Brunings also made arrangements for me to see the Gaines Maplewood farm, where Margaret Garner lived with her children. In addition, I thank the archivists and librarians at the Ohio and Cincinnati Historical Societies. These two institutions have been indispensable to my scholarship throughout my career, and I am forever indebted. The staff members have been generous with their time and have shared information that saved me countless hours of research time. I have noticed that over the years, the staff and services at these two institutions have been reduced in ways that created unnecessary obstacles to my research. I encourage Ohio legislators to recognize why it is *imperative* that they continue to fund these important institutions. I also thank Lance at the Kentucky Department for Libraries and Archives for searching high and low for that requisition order, the Kentucky Historical Society, and the Dallas Public Library for helping me locate copies of the Gaines family Bible.

Although many family members, friends, students, and colleagues have provided moral support throughout my entire career, one person made the difference in my finishing *this* book, my daughter. She embodies what Margaret Garner may have dreamed of for her own daughters: a life pregnant with possibilities, hope, and boundless freedom.

Acknowledgments

INTRODUCTION
Bodies and Souls

Enslaved women rarely used deadly violence in the long history of American slavery. Those who did, typically killed their owners and not their loved ones—especially not their own living, breathing children. In 1856, Margaret Garner, an enslaved woman from northern Kentucky, murdered her infant daughter and attempted to kill her other children while trying to escape slavery. The question this book answers is why. What concerns or grievances led this enslaved woman to commit deadly violence? Margaret Garner's story suggests that damage done to them as women—as wives and mothers, in particular—could and did sometimes drive them to murder.

Margaret Garner's life history is full of things deemed unspeakable, dishonorable, and ugly in nineteenth-century America, including physical abuse, child murder, possible sexual abuse and mental illness, slavery, and death. Her story is as uncomfortable as it is captivating—so much so, that it has inspired several novels, works of historical fiction, collected essays, a film, and an opera. The story had completely dropped out of the public consciousness and conscience for more than one hundred years until Toni Morrison reintroduced it through her 1987 novel *Beloved*. The novel and Jonathan Demme's 1998 film adaptation with the same name, starring Oprah Winfrey, Danny Glover, and Thandie Newton, helped raise the public consciousness about this tragic story. Set after the Civil War just outside Cincinnati, Ohio, *Beloved* is about a former slave woman named

Sethe who beheaded her own two-year-old daughter to prevent her from being sent back to slavery. Sethe is haunted by the angry ghost of her murdered daughter until that spirit is made flesh in a young woman who shows up at her door one day. The arrival of the young woman leads Sethe on a path whereby she is forced to confront the painful memories and traumas of her enslaved past. Morrison's *Beloved* is a powerful assertion that slavery damaged not only black women's exteriors—their bodies—but also their interiors—their minds and spirits.

Driven toward Madness: The Fugitive Slave Margaret Garner and Tragedy on the Ohio uses the real history of Garner to demonstrate how slavery can and did cause interior and exterior injuries. This book reminds the reader in painstaking detail what life must have been like for Margaret Garner as a powerless, unprotected, and enslaved black woman who bore children in slavery. Such women not only endured various forms of physical and sexual abuse but were susceptible to the emotional traumas of living under the constant threat of violence, rape, familial separation, persistent racist insults, and other forms of degradation. Slavery guaranteed that these women perpetually lived in a state of vulnerability, fear, and physical and emotional pain. Enslaved women mostly endured that damage quietly and internally, but at times, their response erupted violently, outwardly and even publicly, in ways that defy comprehension or prevent our sympathy. This book is concerned with those eruptions of deadly violence and their implications about enslaved women's damaged interiors. It is also concerned with a socially unacceptable type of slave resistance and what it may suggest about enslaved women's power or powerlessness.

Slavery caused trauma. The human responses to that trauma are the concerns of this project. Margaret Garner's case underscores the fact that those responses are not always rational or bloodless. Some of these responses to trauma are, in fact, gruesome and incomprehensible, as hers were. It is easy to conclude that she was mentally ill, but by doing so, we redirect the conversation away from the conditions and experiences that may have triggered such acts, as well as away from the political import of said actions. Margaret Garner resisted in dozens of ways throughout the course of this case and managed, ever so faintly, to tell her very powerful story.

Unfortunately, psychological and spiritual injuries rarely attract the attention of historians. Because the spirit and soul are considered the realm of the metaphysical or spiritual, intellectuals often discount or dismiss injuries to them. Yet there is a direct relationship between racist and sexist insults, sexual and physical assaults—injustice in any form—and psychological pain. The multiplicative and compounded effects of those injuries can "murder" the soul. Historian Nell Irvin Painter, borrowing from the discipline of psychology, uses an interpretive concept of "soul murder," which is a useful framework to explain the experiences of enslaved woman in general and Margaret Garner specifically. According to Nell Painter, sexual abuse, emotional deprivation, physical and mental torture can be "compounded . . . as a series of hurts the weight of which shatters, or wounds, the soul." Soul murder, then, is manifest in depression, anxiety, self-mutilation, or suicide attempts, or the equivalent of what psychologists call posttraumatic stress disorder.[1]

Historian Wilma King asserts that soul murder can make survivors self-destructive or can lead to expressions of extreme hatred toward or a desire to hurt the abuser or violence against others.[2] In other words, soul-murdered people can be driven to actions that are often desperate, violent, irrational, or deadly, like murder. This psychoanalytical framework better explains Margaret Garner's actions than any other. The concept of soul murder is, by no means, an attempt to excuse or justify those actions, but to better understand them. For example, through this framework, one can better understand why she attempted to kill her children instead of Archibald K. Gaines—the man who owned her. Nor is soul murder an attempt to posthumously psychoanalyze Margaret Garner. Instead, the soul murder conceptual framework simply positions physical, sexual, and mental trauma, abuse, and torture as central to this story of slavery, escape, and resistance. Slavery caused real human beings to suffer in various ways, some of which were measurable and others of which were not evident until an eruption of violence occurred. Trauma theory, then, can produce a historical, political, and cultural understanding of the physical and emotional injuries that enslaved women such as Garner suffered.

This book also grapples with the history of black corporality as it intersects with slavery. The late historian Stephanie M. H. Camp in *Closer to Freedom* crafted a brilliant interpretive framework that is quite useful in explaining Margaret Garner's enslavement. Camp contended that enslaved people figuratively possessed three "bodies," or three ways that they experienced slavery corporally. The "first body" was a site of domination and mastery. It is in this body that they were sexually and physically abused and commodified. This book explores ways in which enslaved people were owned and rented, worked and driven, beaten and abused, injured and broken. In addition to those experiences, Garner's dominated body—especially her work productivity and reproductivity—enlarged her owner's wealth, status, and power. Camp's "second body" insists that the body functioned as "a vehicle of terror, humiliation and pain." Garner was soul murdered in her "second body." Camp's "third" body, as a source of pleasure and enjoyment in the face of bondage, is not relevant to this project.[3] If we expand the concept of three bodies, we might consider a fourth body: one that engages in resistance and violent eruptions in response to trauma. *Driven toward Madness* privileges Margaret Garner's corporal slave experience in her first and second body and her response to it in her fourth. In particular, it underscores the abuse, trauma, fear, terror, grief, brokenness, and hopelessness that led to her soul murder while enslaved in Richwood, Kentucky, while also emphasizing the hope of escape and freedom and the subsequent disappointment and desperation when faced with recapture.

This book also uses Margaret Garner's story to underscore how slavery damaged African American women in their roles as women, wives, and mothers. As Patricia Hill Collins has argued, "African-American women's experiences as mothers have been shaped by the dominant group's effort to harness black women's sexuality and fertility to a system of capitalist exploitation." Moreover, slavery despoiled how Margaret Garner practiced motherhood; it despoiled her image of herself as a mother, damaged her bonds with her children, denied her the right to protect them, and even undermined her authority over them. In sum, slavery corrupted everything about motherhood and prevented a full expression of the ideals of womanhood. It also damaged black marriages and families and troubled the bonds between family members. Slavery tried to make a mockery of the Garners' marriage: it refused their rights to live under the same roof or fully enjoy the intimate bonds of marriage when and how they desired. Slavery destroyed the confidence that a child born to a wife was her husband's child. In short, slavery debased Margaret Garner's family inside and out.[4]

My overarching goal is to bring the historical Margaret Garner and her family into sharper focus by underscoring their trauma, as a unit and as individuals. As an enslaved woman, she left only faint traditional historical footprints herself: she could not read or write and left no diary, letters, or personal papers. None of this was her choice, but was a consequence of enslavement. So it is exceedingly difficult to know exactly what she thought or believed. Perhaps this is why Steven Weisenburger concluded in *Modern Medea* that her life was "nonnarratable" until she escaped Kentucky and committed murder.[5]

We would be remiss to accept that the story of this enslaved and traumatized woman is "nonnarratable" until she did something unthinkable. This book provides one example for how we might fill the gaps and silences in historical sources—not with fiction, but with traditional and nontraditional historical sources, other disciplines, methods, and interpretive frameworks. Although Margaret Garner is one of the few runaway slaves ever to testify at his or her own fugitive slave hearing, there are no extant official transcripts of that hearing. Hence, this book relies on the transcriptions of the proceedings of the fugitive slave hearing recorded in the local newspapers, other newspaper accounts, indictment and requisition orders, as well as the manuscript collection of John Pollard Gaines, Margaret's original owner. I utilize interdisciplinary approaches to bring the real Margaret into sharper focus. Anchored in history, this book also makes use of black feminist theory, trauma studies, pain studies, genetics, history of emotions, and literary criticism. Each of these approaches sews a layer of flesh onto a figure who has been rendered an apparition by the sources and raises the decibels of a voice that had been silenced before and after the murder. At the end of this book, a real-life woman in her proper historical and cultural context should emerge. In these critical ways and others, this book differs from Weisenburger's imaginative and entertaining narrative in *Modern Medea,* which mixes history, drama, and historical fiction. *Driven toward Madness* has defied naysayers and journeyed to some difficult historical places to find the real Margaret Garner. It may not definitively answer all of the questions concerning her life, but it gets us a step closer. More than anything, though, this book should simply serve as a guide for how we might reclaim black women's voices and agency in history when traditional historical sources are scarce, nonexistent, vague, coded, or erased.

A black feminist interpretation of Garner's life—as an enslaved woman, wife, and mother—offers a more holistic picture of who she truly was and what drove her to kill. It rejects the distortions and fictionalized images of her that essentially reduce her to various symbols—all with their own audiences and purposes: to free African Americans and abolitionists, Margaret Garner was the first widely known black female hero—a potent symbol of slave resistance; contemporary women's rights advocates tried to use Garner as a feminist symbol; and proslavery folks raised her as a black bogeyman. The real Margaret Garner is nothing close to any of those depictions. Although she had not intended to make a political statement about slavery or women's rights when she attacked her children, her actions are loaded with political meaning, nonetheless. For one, they impugn her owner as particularly cruel and directly undermine the myth that her enslavement had been mild. Beyond simply emphasizing that she was a whole woman and not just a symbol created by others, interdisciplinary theories and approaches allow me to probe slavery's legacy of violence—sexual and physical—and psychic trauma and their capacity to render Margaret Garner "mad." I deal with her as a traumatized black female in historical, social, cultural, and political terms; she carried a history of the trauma of slavery—personal, collective, and compounded—with her on her journey to freedom the day she escaped. Margaret's history of abuse, enslavement, and denied freedom and humanity burdened her with its full weight as she faced her deepest fear of returning to that life and watching her children grow up in it. Despite such burdens and traumas, Margaret Garner was not destroyed and nor was her spirit. Her family and her hope for freedom for her children were a salve.

Garner's trauma is at the center of my historical question, so I find it useful to embrace the history of emotions' assumption that emotions have their own histories. Understanding the historical, social, and cultural context in which these emotional events are produced does get us a step closer to understanding them. How Margaret processed her slave experience, grief, threat of recapture, imprisonment, trial, and subsequent loss on the Ohio River has meaning and significance to this story. Moreover, the history of emotions frees me to make claims about Margaret Garner's emotions based on my familiarity with her world, life, family, words, and actions. As historian Andrew J. Huebner posits, "Evoking feeling does not have to distract us from our primary goal as historians—to convey the character of human life in the past—and in fact helps achieve it."[6]

African American women's history—especially this black woman's history—brings together the history of emotions, the history of black corporality, trauma studies, the histories of science and psychology, legal, political, and social history, the history of slavery, and even the history of free blacks. In short, African American women are at the heart of American history and its many subfields.

"HOPE FLED"

Then, said the mournful mother,
If Ohio cannot save,
I will do a deed for freedom,
Shalt find each child a grave.

I will save my precious children
From their darkly threatened doom,
I will hew their path to freedom
Through the portals of the tomb.

—Frances Ellen Watkins Harper, 1857[1]

Late in the evening of 27 January 1856, the Garners—an extended family of eight people living on two farms in northern Kentucky and ranging in ages from nine months to fifty-five years—escaped from slavery. The fugitive family included twenty-two-year-old Peggy Garner, who was pregnant; her twenty-seven-year-old husband, Simon Jr., also known as "young Simon"; their four children, Tommy, Sammy, Mary, and Cilla—who were almost six, four, and two years, and nine months old, respectively; and young Simon's parents, Simon and Mary, both in their midfifties. Peggy and the children were owned by Archibald K. Gaines of Richwood, and Simon Jr. and his parents lived roughly a mile away, on a farm owned by James Marshall. What made the Garners unusual is not that they escaped slavery, but that they did so as an intact family unit.

Thousands of enslaved people attempted to escape slavery every year in the antebellum era (roughly the years from 1830 to 1860), but only a small fraction succeeded. Coming up with a plan of escape, including the means and route of escape, was incredibly challenging for enslaved people. Even a solid escape plan often was not enough to guarantee success; would-be fugitives had to summon a high degree of courage to face the prospect of permanently leaving behind their farms, families, and communities in pursuit of an uncertain freedom in an unknown region. Only the most ingenious, resourceful, determined, courageous, and fortunate fugitives made it to freedom.

Despite how courageous, empowered, resourceful, and determined the Garners were, and how intensely they desired freedom, the sheer size of their party proved to be a hindrance. Larger groups, with few exceptions, rarely made it to freedom. The larger the group, the greater the risks of discovery and capture.[2] Most potential runaways knew the risks and would not dare attempt to escape with their entire family in tow. The Garners were an exception.

Not only were entire family units unlikely to escape slavery, but even as individuals the Garners were the unlikeliest of runaways. Most runaways tended to be young men in their teens and twenties, traveling alone. None of the Garners fit that profile except Simon Jr. In their mid-fifties, young Simon's parents were the antithesis of that youthful profile. Peggy was well into her fifth pregnancy and certainly could not have made the journey without the assistance of her family. As women and mothers, Peggy and Mary were far from typical runaways, as well, because enslaved women did not commonly try to escape slavery. It is not that these women did not *want* to escape, but because they were the primary caregivers for their children, the thought of leaving them behind was unimaginable; the thought of taking the children with them was equally overwhelming. In other words, children decreased the likelihood that their mothers would escape. Interestingly enough, although women did not escape bondage as often as men, most of those who did were driven out of a fear of losing their children through sale, and those took the children with them.[3]

Gender ideals and obligations to family and community kept enslaved women tied to their farms and plantations. Ideals about black womanhood pressured women not to leave their children behind if they did flee:

the culture dictated that mothers should be selfless and sacrificing. Good mothers, then, did not abandon their children, just as good wives did not abandon their husbands, on a quest for personal freedom. Additionally, enslaved women had fewer realistic opportunities to escape because of their relatively limited mobility. Nineteenth-century gender conventions limited the movements of enslaved African American women and confined them where they lived and worked. They were subjected to what the historian Stephanie Camp termed a "geography of containment." The only exceptions were those women who traveled with their owner's family as personal servants or nurses. By comparison, enslaved men possessed far more mobility than enslaved women: they transported products to the market, did errands, carried messages for their owners, worked in cities, and sometimes worked jobs for pay. Moreover, they were more likely to be given passes to visit family members. Enslaved women's geography of containment was certainly true for the Garner women. Peggy claimed she had been to Cincinnati only once—as a small girl—underscoring how little mobility she had had in her entire life. Mary Garner had been hired out once about five years before the escape; she then spent a year hired out to a man named Cas Warrington, of Covington, Kentucky—a small town just across the river from Cincinnati. During her service to Warrington, Mary enjoyed mobility for the first time in her life. He often sent her to Cincinnati on errands and allowed her to travel there by herself to attend church services. But it had been years since she had enjoyed that mobility. By contrast, young Simon had been hired out several times and had frequently traversed Boone County, northern Kentucky, and Cincinnati, so he was quite familiar with the regional geography. He knew the location of the toll roads—manned by guards ready to sound an alarm about runaways—and how to avoid them. Simon Jr. knew just where farmland met streams or steep hills and where the bends in the road could obscure travelers. These gendered differences of mobility mattered because regional geographical familiarity—especially in the dark—proved essential to successfully navigate the family to freedom.[4]

Women were unlikely runaways for another reason: they rarely had the opportunity to disappear or absent themselves from work for any period of time without being missed immediately. On farms, the distinction of the work duties between those who worked in the house and those who worked in the fields was not as sharp as it was on large plantations. Enslaved women on farms did farmwork and housework. In addition to tending to crops and animals, these women cooked, cleaned, sewed, and nursed—or babysat—children for their owners. They worked virtually around the clock, meeting all sorts of demands and needs of members of the slave-owning family and their guests. And these women could hope for little reprieve from the on-call, around-the-clock work regimen, because their work and home spaces often were practically the same sites. Many owners of small farms could not afford to have separate structures for their enslaved workers, so they often lived in the main family structures, in the kitchens or other auxiliary rooms.[5] Hence, living in such close quarters to whites, these women would be quickly missed if they escaped.

Most slaves who seriously contemplated running away understood that traveling with children posed huge challenges that exponentially decreased the odds of their success. The ages and number of children could make an already difficult journey even more conspicuous and trying. Infants, especially, had to be wrapped well to protect them from the extreme elements. The risks included frostbite, heat stroke, dehydration, exhaustion, and illness. Adults had to carry infants and small children whose legs could not handle the walking. Moreover, at any given point, infants and toddlers could, without warning, cry into the darkness, alerting sleeping owners or the slave patrol that someone was escaping. Understandably, few escaping with young babies or small children in tow were successful.[6] Moreover, traveling with one child was difficult enough; more than two children made such journeys exercises in futility. Yet the Garners had four very young children, including an infant and a toddler. Given these odds, how did the Garners have the audacity to escape?

Enslaved people in Kentucky did not have as robust a history of plotting or executing slave rebellions as other slave states, although at least one completed revolt and a handful of significant plots occurred there.[7] One possible explanation is that in Kentucky enslaved people were outnumbered by whites nearly four to one, scattered across the countryside, and often enslaved on farms with only one, two, or three others.[8] On smaller farms and homesteads, enslaved people spent more time with whites, leaving little opportunity to gather as a community to air common grievances or to plot insurrection. In antebellum Kentucky, it was far more common for enslaved people to resist slavery through insolence, defiance, or covert forms of resistance like work slowdowns or feigning illness—in other words, individual acts not designed to overthrow the institution or permanently shed their slave status. Not content with those options, the Garners wanted a certain and final break from slavery altogether.

What were the probabilities of slaves securing freedom in Boone County, Kentucky—legitimately, or otherwise? Geography created the best biggest threat to the security of slavery in northern Kentucky. Boone County was close enough to Ohio, a free state, that slave owners faced the likely possibility of their slaves escaping at any point. Besides that, there were cross-state relationships that further increased the likelihood of escape. Many enslaved people in Boone County had free relatives living in Cincinnati who could facilitate their escape or hide them. Slaveholders with only a handful of slaves could not afford to lose any to escape, making them more controlling and watchful over the movements of their bondspeople. Consequently, enslaved people in that area found that freedom was hard to come by—either through escape or manumission. In 1850, twelve Boone County slaves managed to escape slavery and another eight were manumitted—six of whom were freed by the same person.[9] Taken together, only twenty African Americans—1 percent—obtained their freedom in that county that year. That is just a small snapshot of the dim dream of freedom in Boone County despite its proximity to a free state.

The Garners were undeterred by the odds. They had a clear vision of freedom and a mental roadmap of how to get there. Freedom was not an abstraction for them: a few of the Garner adults had been to Cincinnati and witnessed how free and freed African Americans lived. For example, Mary Garner said that when she was hired out in northern Kentucky, she had sometimes attended the Cincinnati AME church. Her experience in an independent black church—and an AME one at that—introduced her to a vibrant free black community that practiced a liberatory version of Christianity. Although she had been a Christian for two decades, there were no black churches in Richwood or Boone County, where they lived as slaves. Those experiences in the Cincinnati church undoubtedly affected her spirituality, view of bondage, and desire for freedom.[10] Nor was freedom an ideal or remote fantasy for the Garners. Freedom was not a distant place outside of their grasp or awareness; freedom was sixteen miles away, and they knew the route.

A successful escape required careful planning, coordinated efforts, resources, advance knowledge of the geography and terrain, and the assistance of free blacks. The Garner escape was not impulsive; it was the result of at least a month of careful planning and coordination. Young Simon was the engine behind the entire scheme. Although they all collectively decided that they would escape, he made all the plans and supplied every resource they needed, including geographical knowledge, transportation, a pistol for protection, and a safe house.

The escape plan hinged on making contact with black Cincinnati because the family needed people to assist them on the other side of the Ohio River. This support was critical: fugitive slaves with friends and kin in free states who were willing to provide assistance had better chances of success. In December 1855, Simon Jr. had accompanied Thomas W. Marshall, the nineteen-year-old son of his owner, to Cincinnati to drive hogs in for slaughter and sale, as he had done so many times before. The men had grown up at the same time and may have played together as children. Of the relationship, Thomas Marshall said that he had always treated young Simon as more of a companion than a slave. But by the time they were adults, few would have defined them as friends—largely because the racial and status boundaries between them had hardened, creating an unbridgeable gulf. For Simon Jr. this trip's significance had nothing to do with work or male bonding; indeed, the trip proved to be a crucial factor in finalizing the Garners' plans to escape. During that December trip, Thomas made the critical mistake of giving Simon Jr. some freedom to visit his wife's relatives, Sarah and Joseph Kite. The Kites' son, Elijah, was Peggy's first cousin. Peggy, young Simon, and Elijah had spent some portion of their childhoods together in the same Richwood neighborhood before Elijah escaped in 1850.[11]

After taking leave of his young owner, Simon Jr. had inquired of several African Americans on the street where to find Joseph and Sarah Kite's home. Most African Americans living in Cincinnati then knew who Joseph Kite was and where he lived. A man named Edward John Wilson directed young Simon to the Kite home on Sixth Street, east of Broadway, near the Bethel AME Church.[12]

Joseph Kite had been born into bondage on March 16, 1787, in Culpeper Court House, Virginia, where he spent the first sixteen years of his life. By the time he was thirty years old, his owner relocated to east Tennessee. Joseph eventually ended up in Boone County, Kentucky—likely owned by George Kite of Burlington, who had an enslaved workforce of seven. In Boone County, Joseph had met his wife, Sarah, who was nearly twenty years his junior. They had at least one child together, Elijah. Joseph hired his own time and earned enough money to eventually purchase his freedom in 1825. He immediately moved to Cincinnati, joining a heavy stream of African Americans who shed their slave status, legally or otherwise, and settled in Cincinnati, "Queen City of the West," in the 1820s. Joseph Kite bore the distinction of being among only a small number of African Americans who lived in the city before the great exodus of 1829, when impending mob violence precipitated the historic exodus of half of the black population. Here, at least, jobs abounded to nearly the same extent as the racism and legal proscriptions black settlers faced. Joseph Kite worked as a peddler for many years.[13] Although not considered entirely respectable work, the entrepreneurial nature of peddling worked in his favor; he soon had saved enough to purchase his wife and contracted with Wilson Harper, his son Elijah's owner, to purchase him for $450. Elijah escaped in 1850 with his wife and their five-year-old child before the transaction was complete, though. Now a fugitive slave, Elijah settled in central Ohio for a few years and then moved to Cincinnati to be nearer to his parents. When Harper learned of Elijah's whereabouts, he chose not to retrieve him under the 1850 Fugitive Slave Act, but decided, instead, to take a gamble and sue Joseph Kite for breach of contract regarding the broken purchase agreement. Joseph Kite hired abolitionist attorney John Jolliffe to defend him, who persuasively argued that the contract was nullified because it had been drawn up in Ohio, where laws prohibited any buying and selling of slaves.[14]

A thirty-year resident of one of the most racist cities in antebellum America, Joseph Kite had witnessed more than his fair share of mobs and near mobs. However, he also had witnessed much good in Cincinnati, including the establishment of several of the city's first black churches and schools, as well as the growth and stabilization of the black community. He was a pillar of that community. Kite had lived in the city long enough to see the Underground Railroad grow from a few committed free blacks who risked life and limb, to a strong interracial network stretching across several Ohio counties. Joseph and his son, Elijah, knew the inner workings of the Cincinnati Underground Railroad and who the main conductors were. Even if they were not operatives in that movement, they became de facto activists when their own kin made the decision to seek their assistance. Simon Jr. reasoned that the location of the elder Kites' home—in a very populated section of town in the heart of the black community—was too conspicuous. Besides that, everyone knew Joseph. Elijah, however, lived in a less dense part of town in the western section of the city. Simon Jr. weighed the likelihood of capture at both homes and decided he would take his family to Elijah Kite's residence once they crossed the Ohio River.

During his Christmas visit with Peggy's relatives, young Simon had familiarized himself with the exact location of the home at Sixth and Mill Streets. He remained with the Kites for two days and even enjoyed a Christmas play before meeting up with Thomas Marshall to make the journey back to Richwood. That visit ensured him that they had a destination and capable support on the other side of the river and allowed him to finalize the family's plans to flee.

Young Simon might have claimed his own freedom then, based on his stay in Ohio. State laws protected black freedom for those legally on its soil. According to the 1841 *State v. Farr* ruling, an enslaved person brought into Ohio willingly by his or her owner, even with the intention of simply passing through it, was considered free.[15] He could have taken advantage of Thomas's mistake of bringing him into the state and boldly claimed his freedom in a court of law and won. Joseph Kite's abolitionist attorney, John Jolliffe, would have made certain of that. Moreover, had young Simon absconded then, he could have easily put himself into the capable hands of Underground Railroad agents—never to return to bondage or Boone County. Instead, he made the selfless, but ill-fated, decision not to pursue freedom without his family, so he returned to Kentucky with Thomas Marshall.[16]

The Garners waited nearly three weeks to escape after Simon Jr.'s return to Richwood. Perhaps they did not have an earlier opportunity. When the opportunity did present itself, the family coordinated the departure of Peggy and her children, Tommy, Sammy, Mary, and Cilla, who lived on the Gaines farm, named Maplewood, and Simon Jr. and his parents, Mary and Simon, who lived on James Marshall's property. Timing was critical: they had to wait until all their owners had retired to bed on the night they planned to leave. They also had to be careful not to leave too early, lest they awaken the sleeping families with the slightest sound; yet they also had to leave enough time to travel the sixteen miles to Cincinnati, which was a day's journey by foot under normal circumstances. The Garners knew there was no way they could have made the long journey by foot—especially with four small children and with Peggy being pregnant.

Moreover, the sixteen miles between their farms in Boone County, Kentucky, and freedom in Cincinnati, Ohio, would seem like a thousand in freezing temperatures. So Simon Jr. found transportation for the family of eight: a sleigh and two old horses from the Marshall farm to pull it. He and his parents brought the horse-drawn sleigh over to Maplewood to collect Peggy and the children at 10:00 p.m. on 27 January 1856.[17]

The night of 27 January was exceptionally frigid—cold enough that the Ohio River was frozen. Conventional wisdom would lead one to question why the Garners left in the winter with its frigid temperatures and snowy, icy conditions; but the warmer months actually posed more obstacles to travel and risks of discovery. First, more people would have been outside in the evening in the warmer months, ensuring that someone would have seen the fugitive family along the way. Second, there would have been no way to convey a party that size and with such small children in warmer weather; they would have had to walk. The sleigh across snow made travel infinitely easier and faster than walking. Finally, in warmer months, the Ohio River, which separated the slave south from the free north, would have been a barrier to freedom, because they would have needed a boat or skiff to get across. It would have been exceedingly difficult to find someone willing to ferry them across because Kentucky laws forbade ferryman from carrying African Americans across the river without a permit from their owners.[18] Moreover, the fugitives would have needed a boat big enough for eight—an unlikely prospect.

One advantage of having worked in such proximity to the river for all those years is that the Simon Jr. knew its particularities. For example, in the nineteenth century, those who knew anything about the Ohio River knew it frequently froze solid in January and February; and when it did, it became a natural bridge from the slave state of Kentucky to the free state of Ohio. This knowledge was invaluable to the fugitives and dictated when they escaped. In sum, it actually was wiser and easier to flee in the winter.

The journey took the family all night. The fugitives likely would have stayed off of the main tolls roads lest they be discovered by toll guards. Instead, they likely would have taken farm roads and open fields to avoid the guards, who would have sounded the alarm. We can only speculate about what delayed them, but a couple of old horses pulling an entire family of eight through snow would have been a hard tow. The long journey pushed the horses to their limits—the animals barely finishing the task of towing the weight of eight people the sixteen miles to the riverbank in frigid temperatures. The Garners abandoned the horses and sleigh at Washington House, a Covington hotel, and walked the last few hundred feet to the edge of the frozen Ohio River close to the Walnut Street Ferry. There, they faced another obstacle: crossing the half-mile-wide river undetected. Police watchmen were supposed to keep close watch of the river to ensure that fugitive slaves did not cross. Young Simon had lived in northern Kentucky, so he would have been familiar with the location of the watchmen's posts.

After getting past night watchmen, the Garners' next obstacle was moving across the ice, an unnatural walking surface, especially in the dark. Each of the adults would have carried a child across the river, since all but one was too small to navigate the ice without slipping and falling: Tommy, the oldest child, may have walked on his own. Each step the Garners took would have collectively put thousands of pounds of pressure onto the icy surface. Any misstep on a fragile section of the ice could have cracked it, sending some or all of the Garners to an icy death. The drama of an enslaved mother crossing the frozen Ohio River with her child in her arms was not a new one. The character Eliza in *Uncle Tom's Cabin* is based on the real woman, Eliza Harris, who also escaped slavery and ran across the frozen river years before Peggy Garner.[19] In fact, we will probably never know how many other enslaved mothers made the same perilous decision to cross the icy river on foot.

As they crossed the frozen Ohio River, the Garners shed their slave status and put on the mantle of freedom. The younger couple decided to assume new names, which served the triple functions of hiding their real identities, distancing themselves from their enslaved pasts, and claiming new destinies on free soil. And apparently, it was fairly common for fugitive slaves to choose new names in freedom. Peggy assumed her formal name Margaret (Peggy is the common nickname for Margaret); like his wife, Simon Jr. may have adopted a formal birth name or even a middle name when he chose to be called Robert. The couple's four children and young Simon's parents retained their names. Peggy and Simon Jr. would walk into the annals of history bearing their freedom names of Margaret and Robert.[20]

The Garners made it to the Cincinnati riverbank after sunrise on 28 January—hours later than they had hoped. Unfortunately, sunrise increased the risks of someone seeing them. Still, they pressed onward. Robert led his family to a house at Sixth and Mill Streets in the western part of the city, four houses from the Mill Creek Bridge. Their journey finally ended at around 8:00 a.m., some grueling ten hours after it had begun, at the home of Margaret's cousin, Elijah Kite, and his wife, Mary.[21]

When they arrived, the Garners were tired, hungry, and cold. Kite welcomed his cousin and her family and introduced them to his wife, who began preparing their breakfast. The family decided it best to move to a more secure location immediately after breakfast. To that end, Kite hastily left to consult with Levi Coffin, a Quaker Underground Railroad operative, about how to move the large family to a safer location. As a white man, Coffin not only had more experience with large parties of fugitive slaves but also enjoyed civil rights that would safeguard against anyone barging into his home, searching it without a warrant, or seizing any occupants. As an African American, Kite did not enjoy these rights. Besides that, by harboring his cousin and her family, he risked a $1,000 fine and a six-month imprisonment under the 1850 Fugitive Slave Act. In a city like Cincinnati, which had a long history of antiabolitionist violence, Kite also risked being targeted by a mob. Coffin advised him to move the family further up Mill Creek to a black settlement that routinely harbored fugitives.[22] After leaving Coffin's house, Kite hurried back to his own home intending to follow his advice. Unfortunately, shortly after he returned home, he got some unexpected visitors.

Archibald K. Gaines, the owner of Margaret and the children, had discovered the family was missing only a few hours after they left Richwood and had gone after them with dogged determination. Before getting on the road to Cincinnati, he had gone over to the Marshall farm to see if the rest of the Garner family had escaped. There, the slave-owning neighbors learned that the entire family indeed had left, taking a sleigh and two horses with them. Marshall, who was too ill to travel, sent his son Thomas to retrieve his slaves.

Gaines and young Marshall quickly closed the distance between themselves and the fugitive family. It was not hard to follow the clues the Garners had left along the way, including the sleigh and horses left abandoned in Covington. Gaines and Marshall knew that the Garners' kin, Joseph and Sarah Kite, resided somewhere in Cincinnati. Moreover, Thomas Marshall would have remembered that Robert had gone to visit them late the previous year. After some inquiries, someone directed the pursuers to Elijah Kite's street. There, a girl pointed out the home and informed them that the party had gone inside.[23]

Once they knew the family's location, the slaveholders left someone to watch the home while they went to secure a warrant under the 1850 Fugitive Slave Act from John L. Pendery, the United States Commissioner for the Southern District of Ohio. The provisions of that law granted slaveholders authority to retrieve runaways in free states. It also provided for the appointment of federal commissioners, or officers, in local communities throughout the nation who were charged with enforcing the law. The 1850 Fugitive Slave Act outlined a clear process for owners to reclaim fugitive slaves: Upon discovering the whereabouts of their slave, owners had to go before a commissioner who could issue a warrant for the alleged fugitive's arrest. The federal commissioner would then deputize citizens, bystanders, and posses to help execute the warrants. The law stated that "all good citizens [were] hereby commanded to assist in the prompt and efficient execution of this law."[24] Once in custody, the accused runaway would be brought back to the commissioner for a hearing. The burden of proof for the owner was very low: the only requirement for a person to establish ownership was a witness or affidavit from someone in the home state attesting to the fugitive's identity. In this case, Gaines and Marshall would serve as each other's witness. The 1850 Fugitive Slave Act outlined harsh penalties for those who interfered with, or failed to enforce the law, with federal criminal charges, a fine up to $1,000, or civil lawsuits for the value of the slave. Moreover, the law provided commissioners with a decent incentive to rule in favor of the claimant: commissioners who remanded an African American to slavery were paid $10 and those who ruled in favor of the alleged fugitive received only $5. In current terms, that is equivalent to $247 versus $123. Some interpreted the unequal rewards as an attempt to bribe commissioners. Abolitionists and African Americans believed the 1850 Fugitive Slave Act to be wholly corrupt and designed to benefit slaveholders.[25] That was the grim reality of what the Garners would face should they be recaptured. In sum, they did not stand a chance under this legislation.

After Gaines and Marshall appeared before Commissioner Pendery the morning of 28 January, he promptly issued warrants for the Garners, giving them to John Ellis, the federal marshal, to execute. Pursuant to the provisions of the legislation, Ellis deputized a posse of white men from Cincinnati and northern Kentucky to help execute the warrants. Then the newly deputized marshals, Gaines, and Marshall quickly returned to the Kite home by 10:00 a.m. with warrants in hand, to recover the family. Elijah Kite barely had beaten them back to his home. Apparently, Robert

Garner was none too happy that Elijah had not made arrangements to get the family out of the city ahead of time as they had planned. That fact, plus Elijah's delay at Coffin's house the morning of their arrival, and his return to the home only moments before the marshals arrived led Robert to suspect that he had betrayed the family. It remained a sore spot for Robert until his death.[26] In reality, though, there is no evidence that Elijah had betrayed his cousin and her family to their owners; he may simply have been an ineffective Underground Railroad operative. His missteps, though, canceled the family's herculean efforts to escape slavery.

The Garners were finishing breakfast when the marshals pounded on the locked doors and windows with the authority of the federal government on their side, demanding that they surrender. Mary Kite, Elijah's wife, refused the party entry; Elijah first agreed to let the authorities in but changed his mind.[27] Outside, a crowd—composed of curious passersby, neighbors, proslavery and antislavery sympathizers, deputies, members of the press, and African Americans—gathered around the home and grew larger by the minute.

The deputies tried to force their way into the home. Cornered, the family scrambled, not sure what to do. Robert pulled out a pistol he had taken from his owner to protect his family's freedom. The men had decided to "fight and die" rather than return to slavery. Surely, Robert had freedom and death on his mind as he fired at a deputy who tried to come through a window of the cabin. The bullet hit the deputy, shattering his teeth and leaving his finger hanging "by a mere thread."[28]

The Garner men's decision to resort to armed defense is remarkable for a few reasons. It was a powerful assertion of manhood neither ever had been able to assert in Kentucky: the power to protect their family from everything that had hurt them in the past, plus all that threatened to hurt them outside the doors of that Cincinnati home. Hence, they enacted a type of heroic power that was largely elusive for enslaved men. Moreover, it was a brazen act for African Americans to fire at white men—especially deputized federal authorities—who outnumbered them and had greater firepower. Their decision to use deadly force to avoid capture was not without precedent, though. Other fugitive slaves had used deadly force to avoid capture before the Garners, including in Christiana, Pennsylvania, in 1851. Then, when Maryland slave owner Edward Gorsuch tried to reclaim his slaves from the home of free black William Parker, the armed inhabitants inside shot and killed him and gravely injured his sons.

There were consequences for shooting at white men in the Ohio Valley. Had the shooting occurred across the river in Kentucky, laws there decreed that an enslaved person convicted of maliciously shooting a free white person with the intent to kill could be punished by death, whipping, or imprisonment; a conviction for murdering a white person carried the death penalty.[29] In Ohio, a free state, there were no specific laws against fugitives shooting, injuring, or killing white men, but black on white violence certainly would lead to an extralegal death sentence. African Americans' armed resistance against whites in Cincinnati always prompted swift mob violence against the entire community. None of the consequences deterred Robert from firing a gun against white deputies.

Initially, Margaret, Mary, and the children were in the front room of the Kite home with the Garner men. As Margaret watched the unfolding struggle at the door and became convinced of the inevitability of the family's capture, she grew increasingly agitated, if not panic-stricken, after Robert shot the deputy. She decided to use deadly violence, as well. Grabbing a butcher knife from a counter, she rushed toward her children, grabbing two-year-old Mary and declaring, "Before my children shall be taken back to Kentucky I will kill every one of them!" While the men were trying to keep the posse from gaining entrance, Margaret snatched up two-year-old Mary and quickly cut her throat, right to left. She practically decapitated her daughter with a cut that was estimated to be four or five inches long and three inches deep. She threw the bleeding, dying child to the floor in the corner of the room. Margaret roared to her mother-in-law, "Mother, help me to kill them!" The older woman—the only adult witness to the impending horror—returned, "I cannot help you kill them!" Mary Garner did nothing to stop Margaret from harming her grandchildren; instead, she turned, ran from the room, and hid under a bed in an adjoining room. Not content with taking just one child's life, Margaret then grabbed her sons one at a time and tried cutting their throats. They both fought back, though: one begged for his life, crying, "Oh Mother, do not kill me!" Hearing the commotion and screaming from the boys, Mary and Elijah Kite ran into the front room and witnessed Margaret trying to kill them. Mary Kite rushed over to Margaret and struggled with her for the knife. Tommy and Sammy took that opportunity to run into the next room and hide from their mother under the bed with their grandmother. Once Mary Kite wrested the knife from Margaret, she sternly told her not to kill her children—apparently still unaware that a child already lay

Figure 1.1. Pencil drawing of the Thomas Satterwhite Noble painting *The Modern Medea* (1867). Granger, NYC

bleeding with its neck cut open just a few feet away. Margaret went after the knife a few more times until Mary Kite gave it to her son to put in the privy behind the house.[30]

When the Garner men—who had been occupied preventing the deputies from entering the home—turned and saw what Margaret had done to little Mary, Robert started "screaming, as if bereft of reason," and pacing the room. His anguish was palpable—a testament to how much he loved the little girl. Old Simon groaned, while pacing too, and his wife wept inconsolably. Sheer pandemonium reigned inside the cabin. The men paced and wailed; the boys trembled under a bed—terrified of their own mother; the Garner matriarch cried; and deputies battered in the door, successfully gaining entrance. Meanwhile, as everyone else was focused on the specter of the dying toddler, Margaret, with laser-focused attention, decided to finish her mission. As the marshals battered their way into the now unmanned front door of the home, Gaines instructed the deputies not to do anything illegal. His last directive was that "no harm whatever should be done to the little children." As they burst into the cabin, Robert fired his pistol a few more times at the entering party, but hit no one. Gaines, following behind a marshal, rushed in, grabbed Robert by the wrists, and wrested the pistol away before he could fire another round. Before Margaret could be apprehended, though, she picked up a heavy coal shovel, aiming it at her youngest child, Cilla, who was on the floor in the front room. She managed to bash her daughter in her face with the shovel one time before deputies grabbed it from her. The younger couple reportedly fought the deputies with "the ferocity of tigers" to avoid being taken.[31]

It is important to state here that trauma is not fully digested or comprehended until later. There is a period of latency, and then the trauma of that violence may rush back at once in ways that shock or debilitate the trauma victim. The act of leaving the site of trauma—what Sigmund Freud calls "a form of freedom"—is what accelerates the recognition of the trauma and, ultimately, fosters its eruption. In other words, Margaret's facing recapture and the possibility of returning to her Kentucky enslavement may have led to a rush of traumatic memories and an eruption that resulted in murder.[32] Hence, her trauma—consisting of interior and exterior injuries—is central to understanding what had driven Garner to escape bondage and, when that failed, to commit an infanticidal act.

The family had generational responses to the threat of recapture. The older couple had a quieter, less confrontational response: elder Simon did not use a weapon, and his wife hid under a bed. The younger couple, by contrast, used armed violence to resist returning to the lives they had left. Margaret and Robert each brandished weapons—he a pistol, and she a knife and shovel; neither hesitated even the slightest to use them. The couple gravely injured people in the process of resisting: Robert shot a deputy, while Margaret slit one child from ear to ear, bashed another in the head with a coal shovel, and tried to cut the throats of her other children. The difference in the violence committed by husband and wife is that he turned his weapon outward toward strangers who threatened his family, while Margaret turned hers inward to her own children.

Aggression, public violence, and armed self-defense were understood to be prerogatives of white men in the nineteenth century. Through their violent resistance, the younger Garners exercised a form of power that was a right reserved to white men. The irony is, of course, that as a legally powerless, enslaved woman in a racist and patriarchal society, Margaret had been an object and target of violence her whole life; as a free woman striving to assert her freedom, she became an instrument of deadly violence against someone who was even more powerless than she—an enslaved, female *child*.[33]

With Margaret and the men restrained, the deputies rushed from room to room trying to reclaim the other fugitives. They found the elder Mary Garner hiding under a bed with Tommy and Sammy. When deputies pulled them out, they noticed that Tommy bled from two cuts on his throat—one four inches long—and Sammy from gashes on his head—injuries inflicted by their mother. Cilla's head was swollen and bruised. She bled from her nose as the officials removed her from the Kite home. Someone in the home tenderly wrapped little Mary in a quilt and put her on the bed in the next room. Though cut from ear to ear reportedly, the toddler did not die swiftly. According to witnesses, she gasped and struggled for air as a male neighbor carried her from the bed into the outside yard. She was dying as her parents, grandparents, and siblings were being apprehended, led outside, and loaded into an omnibus, a horse-drawn bus designed to transport groups of passengers in the mid-nineteenth century. As the omnibus carrying her entire family left the scene, little Mary Garner was in the arms of a stranger as she took her last breath.[34] So ended the Garners' quest for freedom. Sadly, their brief freedom in Cincinnati had been marked with violence, much like their bondage.

Still in front of the Kites' home after the omnibus departed, Archibald K. Gaines took Mary's body from the arms of the neighbor, intending to take it back to Covington for a proper burial in a slave cemetery. The crowd vociferously objected to his removing her body before a proper coroner's inquest could be made into her death. Gaines complied and awaited the arrival of Hamilton County Coroner John Menzies, who had been summoned to the home. Coroner Menzies was himself from the same Richwood neighborhood as Gaines and knew the family quite well.[35] He immediately examined the scene and the girl's body, while Gaines patiently waited for him to finish—apparently more concerned about securing Mary's body than securing his other slaves. When Menzies completed his examinations, he gave the toddler's little body back to Gaines, who loaded it, and then proceeded to the Hammond Street jail. A neighbor claimed he held a funeral, but it is not clear where Gaines laid the toddler to rest.[36]

2

BEFORE THE BLOOD

I have but four, the treasures of my soul,
They lay like doves around my heart;
I tremble lest some cruel hand
Should tear my household wreaths apart.

My baby girl, with childish glance,
Looks curious in my anxious eye,
She little knows that for her sake
Deep shadows round my spirit lie.

My playful boys could I forget,
My home night seems a joyous spot,
But with their sunshine mirth I blend
The darkness of their future lot.

—Frances Ellen Watkins Harper, 1857[1]

Mary's death at her own mother's hands cannot be comprehended without going back to the source of the Garners' trauma—the place from which they had run, two farms in Richwood in Boone County, Kentucky, and where the younger couple was known as Peggy and young Simon. Agriculture was the primary economic activity in the state. Kentucky led the South in the production of rye and barley and the raising of horses; it ranked second in the production of hemp, tobacco, corn, wheat, and raising of sheep, and third in hogs. The soil and climate in the Bluegrass State could not yield cotton, rice, or sugarcane; tobacco, though, was prevalent. On the eve of the Civil War, Kentucky produced 25 percent of the nation's total tobacco crops. Throughout most of the early nineteenth century, the state was second only to Virginia in tobacco cultivation, and during the Civil War, Kentucky surpassed Virginia. In Kentucky, 65 percent of the tobacco was produced on small farms—not on plantations, such as the ones in Virginia.[2] As important as tobacco was to Kentucky, the crop played second fiddle to subsistence crops such as corn, rye, and barley.

The small farmers who populated antebellum Kentucky never became as dependent on slave labor as whites in other southern states. Slaveholding simply never became widespread there. For example, in 1850, nearly 77 percent of the adult white males in the state did not own any slaves. Of those who did, their average number of holdings was the fourth smallest in the nation.[3]

Boone County, where the Garners were enslaved, is the northernmost county in Kentucky. In the antebellum era, its rolling hills and plush greenery distinguished its landscape. The county's economy was built by farmers who sold Indian corn, butter, wheat, rye, hay, flax, and hogs. Most farmers sold a diversity of goods ranging from wheat to butter to slaughtered animals. The county ranked second in the state in orchard goods, fifth in wheat, and tenth in hogs. Raising hogs was popular and profitable in Boone County because of its proximity to Cincinnati, or "Porkopolis," a major national pork-packing center. Roughly 40 percent of Boone County farmers who produced these goods depended on slave labor to do so.[4] In 1850, the county boasted 11,185 residents, and more than 19 percent of them, or 2,100, were enslaved—a percentage that is slightly lower than the statewide average. Richwood, the town where the Garners lived, had a significantly higher density of enslaved people than the rest of the county and about double that of the entire state. About half the residents in that small town were enslaved. Without a doubt then, Richwood was a slaving community. Only 485 white households owned Boone County's entire slave population, which averages about four per slaveholding family. Most of the slaveholders in the county were yeoman slaveholders, defined as those who owned fewer than nine slaves (There were a few extremes, though: one Boone County slaveholder owned twenty-five enslaved people.). Only thirty-seven free African Americans lived in the county, making Boone among the counties with the smallest ratio of free blacks in the upper South. The low number of free blacks suggests that it was rare for slaves to be freed or manumitted in that county; and those who were freed, left.[5]

Kentuckians then and now often boasted that slavery was "milder" or more "innocent" in the Bluegrass State than on cotton plantations in the deep South. They wrongly assume that slavery in Kentucky was physically less demanding and grueling, beatings and punishments less brutal, and the destruction of slave families less common. Kentuckians also wrongly assume that slave owners in their state were benevolent patriarchs who treated their bondspeople humanely. Gaines's attorney would later remark that "the slavery of Kentucky is so mild in form that I infinitely prefer it to the poverty of the North." He added, "The condition of slaves in the South is much better . . . than the half-starved free colored people of the North." Whites living in Richwood in the 1850s claimed that the Garners were "well-housed," "well-fed," and looked "contented and happy." They also insisted that the Garners had "always received great kindness" and "the comforts of a family."[6] When the Garners escaped and violently resisted returning to that "mild" slavery, they discredited such fantasies.

No, enslaved Kentuckians did not work in cotton fields in the searing sun from sunup to sundown; nor did they work on rice plantations in humid, malarial conditions, but those facts do not mean their enslavement was "mild." Kentucky slavery had its own brand of hardship and horror. The smaller size of Kentucky farms was a disadvantage for enslaved African Americans, not a benefit. For one, the smaller the number of slaves a farmer owned, the greater the workload for them.

There is a direct relationship between the quantity of work obligations and the quality of life for enslaved people.[7] Those living and working on small farms had to perform farm and household duties. Because of the various livestock and crops being raised and grown at the farm where Peggy lived, her range of chores may have included milking the cows, churning butter, herding sheep, cutting their wool, feeding the animals, collecting firewood, preparing the soil for seeding, planting, and harvesting the crops. In addition, she also may have been responsible for work inside the Gaineses' home, including cooking, cleaning, washing clothes, sewing, and canning food. In addition to farmwork and house duties, enslaved women on small farms would have also been charged with minding the children of their owners. Without a doubt, the work was exhausting and perpetual.

Enslaved Kentuckians would have been on call virtually around the clock, with little privacy or time to themselves. Many did not even have separate living quarters. Added to that misery, those enslaved on small farms had more daily contact with their owners, which proved harmful, in most cases. The greater contact with owners increased the likelihood that they would endure not only more racist verbal insults and physical assaults, but sexual abuse as well. Given their low numbers per farm, Kentucky slaves were geographically isolated from other African Americans. In short, enslaved Kentuckians did not have much access to, or opportunity to participate in, a viable community. Without the comfort and support of a community, despair, isolation, and hopelessness could easily consume them.[8]

Although enslavement on small Kentucky farms clearly was difficult, the disposition and character of the owner trumped all other conditions in determining the quality of bondage. Being overworked, isolated, and overly exposed to indignities were characteristic of slavery on small Kentucky farms. An exacting, abusive, and cruel owner made things worse. To be enslaved on a small farm with such an owner was—as far as the Garner family was concerned—worse than death. The Garners' collective and individual histories teach us that the brutality or mildness of slavery depended not just on the region or the kind of crop enslaved people tended to, but the character of the owner.

THE GAINES FAMILY

Archibald Kinkead Gaines, born 1 January 1808, was the eighth of thirteen children of Susan Elizabeth Mathews (who went by Elizabeth) and Abner LeGrand Gaines. Native Virginians, the Gaineses had migrated to Boone County, Kentucky, in the early nineteenth century. Abner Gaines purchased 236 acres of land, which lay at a transportation junction in Boone County. Soon a small settlement called Gaines Crossroads sprang up near his land. Gaines Crossroads and the town born of it eventually became Walton, Kentucky. Abner operated a farm, a mail stage line, and a tavern that was frequented by travelers en route to Lexington. In addition to running his tavern, he also acted as the town's justice of the peace and sheriff. Upon his death in 1839, Abner left nearly all of his estimated $12,000–$15,000 in wealth to his youngest daughter, including his farm, home, tavern, livestock, and two slaves. He willed the other Gaines children $1,000 each and various keepsakes. Elizabeth, his widow and the family matriarch, inherited only the furniture and a carriage. Shortly after her husband's death, she moved in with their second-oldest son, John Pollard Gaines, at his farm in nearby Richwood.[9]

The Gaineses had a high sense of obligation to one another. Just as John Pollard had done with the family matriarch, other family members took in relatives from time to time. For example, it was not unusual for an uncle to have his niece or nephew in his home for some time. The naming patterns in the Gaines family also reveal that they honored their kin with each birth. Sons were not named after their fathers, as one might expect, but received the first or middle names of an uncle, brother, grandfather, or even family friend. Male names John, Pollard, Abner, and LeGrand were recycled in several generations in various combinations. Similarly, Gaines women were named after their grandmothers or aunts. Matriarchs' maiden names also were utilized. For example, many of Abner and Elizabeth's children, grandchildren, and beyond received the middle name Mathews, which was Elizabeth's maiden name. The only child who was not named in this tradition was Archibald Kinkead Gaines, who was named after Abner's friend, Captain Archibald Kinkead, who lived in Woodford County, Kentucky.[10]

Several of the Gaines men built lucrative careers as attorneys, slave-holders, and politicians. John Pollard Gaines and Richard Mathews Gaines were successful attorneys who also owned lucrative farms and plantations. Richard once had served as the US attorney in Mississippi before relocating to Chicot County, Arkansas, where he owned the Mason Lake cotton plantation. James Mathews Gaines was one of the three wealthiest farmers in Boone County; his farm was valued at $50,000 in 1850 (roughly $25 million today). Another brother, Benjamin Pollard Gaines, owned a 5,000-acre cotton plantation in Chicot County, Arkansas, and seventy-seven slaves, and Abner LeGrand owned a cotton plantation in New Orleans. The Gaines brothers, like their father Abner, made brilliant real estate purchases that happened to lie at transportation crossroads like their father's had. For example, William constructed a shipping landing on his plantation along the Mississippi River in Chicot County, Arkansas, called Gaines Landing, which became one of the busiest shipping ports on the Mississippi River from 1830 through the Civil War. He also pioneered the development of Hot Springs, Arkansas. A couple of other sons built respectable military careers. Most noteworthy is the career of John Pollard Gaines of Richwood, Kentucky, who served in both the War of 1812 and the Mexican War. In the Mexican War, Gaines surrendered to Mexican General José Vicente Miñón at Encarnación in late January 1847 and subsequently was taken as a prisoner of war. When news of his captivity made it back to Boone County, the story had changed to his having been captured—not that he had surrendered. In 1847, the community honored that presumed bravery by electing Gaines to Congress in absentia as a Whig.[11]

Archibald K. Gaines took a more circuitous route to success than his brothers. In his twenties, he moved to St. Tammany Parish, Louisiana, to seek his fortune—probably following a brother or uncle.[12] He returned to Kentucky soon thereafter and was appointed United States Postmaster in Walton on 16 April 1832. This is the same post that previously had been held by his older brother James.[13] The job offered some steady income and respectability, but did not lead to wealth. In 1836, Archibald K. Gaines reputedly served in the Texas Army of Sam Houston during the Battle for Texas Independence. Afterward, he moved to Chicot County, Arkansas, where several of his brothers, Richard Mathews, William Henry, and Benjamin Pollard owned cotton plantations and managed Gaines Landing. Archibald K. Gaines worked as a land agent and may have also helped his brothers manage their plantations.[14]

Archibald married Margaret Ann Dudley of Scott County, Kentucky, on 26 August 1843 and she joined him in Arkansas. That union produced two children, Elizabeth, born in 1844, and John Dudley, born a year and a half later. A third child died in infancy two years later. Then in January 1849 tragedy struck Archibald when Margaret Ann, pregnant with their fourth child, fell down some stairs, receiving grave injuries. The baby was delivered stillborn, but she lingered on a few more days before finally succumbing to her injuries. Margaret's dying wish was that her daughter, Elizabeth, be raised by her mother in Kentucky.[15] Archibald Gaines returned to Kentucky with their two small children shortly after his wife's death, likely to get assistance with raising them.

Around the same time, after serving just one term in Congress (1847–49), John Pollard Gaines—now released from captivity and back in Kentucky—lost his bid for reelection in the fall 1849 elections. Not long after that defeat, President Zachary Taylor appointed him governor of the Oregon Territory. John Pollard promptly sold his farm and his enslaved workforce to his younger brother Archibald, who had recently returned to the area widowed, raising his children alone, and needing a fresh start. John practically gave the farm to his younger brother. The bill of sale between the brothers dated November 1849 indicates that Archibald purchased five bondspeople—including Peggy, Sam, Hannah, Harry, and Charlotte—for $2,500 from his elder brother. Peggy was just sixteen and likely pregnant with her eldest son at the time of the sale.[16] Archibald K. Gaines as a slave master certainly would be a grand experiment.

Widowed and desperately needing help raising his young children, Gaines turned to their aunt Elizabeth Dudley, Margaret's younger sister, for assistance. Elizabeth was a familiar face, and both he and the children trusted her. The relationship between Gaines and his sister-in-law evolved from there, and the couple married at his church in Covington on 2 April 1850, just a little over a year after Margaret's death. Their marriage may be unsettling to our modern sensibilities, but apparently, it was not at all unusual for Kentuckians to marry their deceased wives' sisters, or even their own blood relatives, or in-laws, for that matter. Brothers John Pollard and Benjamin Pollard Gaines, for example, had married two women who were sisters. Endogamy, the practice of marrying a relative, apparently was common among southern elite whites. In general as many as 22 percent of marriages in some white, rural Kentucky communities were between first cousins.[17] Given the pervasiveness of endogamy, Richwood residents would not have raised an eyebrow at Gaines's marriage to his sister-in-law, since they were not blood relatives. The two immediately expanded their family: Margaret Ann (named in honor of Elizabeth's dead sister) was born in 1851, and William Stockton in 1854. Gaines's two sets of children, thus, were first cousins and siblings.

Gaines's farm was a complex enterprise, sitting on 210 acres of land.[18] Its name, Maplewood, was fitting given the farm's many maple trees. In 1850, Gaines raised livestock and grew assorted crops for the market. He owned 11 horses, 21 milch cows (cows used for milk and butter), 4 working oxen, 110 hogs, and 95 sheep. These animals not only worked and fed his family but also produced income. The livestock yielded 90 pounds of wool and 400 pounds of butter in one year. Many of the 110 hogs were raised expressly to be sold in the pork-packing industry in Cincinnati. Maplewood also produced 250 bushels of wheat, 100 bushels of rye, 100 bushels of Irish potatoes, 50 bushels of oats, and 10 bushels of sweet potatoes that year. By far, though, Indian corn was the biggest farm product at Maplewood in 1850, to the tune of 1,200 bushels.[19] Not all the produce at Maplewood was raised for profit. Much of the hay, oats, and corn would have been used to feed the livestock. Many of the bushels of potatoes would have been consumed by the Gaines family and their slaves, along with some of the hogs, since pork and potatoes were staples in southern diets then. Most of the wheat was produced for commercial purposes, as were the hogs (for cured hams and bacon), sheep (for mutton and merino wool), and milch cows. Maplewood was an extremely valuable farm in 1850, worth $15,000, placing it in the top twenty of the county's most valuable farms. The value of that farm today would be $470,000. Certainly, that level of wealth elevated Archibald's social position, respect, prestige, and honor in his community. By 1860, Maplewood's value had ballooned to $26,000, which is equivalent to $814,000 today.[20] Although Gaines had not built his wealth on his own, the value of Maplewood in 1850 and 1860 placed him in the top echelon of Boone County's farmers.

Gaines's wealth was determined not just by the value of his farm; the number of enslaved persons a slaveholder owned also mattered. In fact, enslaved persons were the crucial "building blocks of a planter's way of life, social mobility, and self-conceptions."[21] In 1850, Archibald K. Gaines owned just nine slaves, classifying him as one of Boone County's numerous yeoman slaveholders. His enslaved workforce of nine included five women, aged fourteen to thirty-two; two adult males, twenty-four and twenty-five years old; and two boys, a preteen and a five-month-old infant male—likely Peggy's oldest son, Thomas, also known as Tommy. Gaines depended on the labor of the five enslaved women, who were in their prime working and reproductive years. In fact, his wealth directly depended not only on black women's productivity at Maplewood, but also on their *re-productivity*. Still, with nine bondspeople in 1850, Gaines ranked among the top 13 percent of slaveholders in Boone County—even as a yeoman. There was nothing exceptional about him, Maplewood, or his choices in crops that promised he would be anything other than a yeoman slaveholder into perpetuity. Yet a year later, he owned twelve bonds people, moving him to the top 4 percent of all slaveholders in Boone County.[22] In short, the reproductivity of the women Gaines owned quickly catapulted him from the ranks of yeoman slaveholders to small planters—technically defined as those who owned between ten and twenty slaves. It was a meteoric rise by Kentucky standards. But being a successful farmer was one thing, and a successful slave owner quite another.

Considering the size of his enslaved workforce, the value of his farm, and his family prominence, Archibald K. Gaines had the trappings and appearance of a member of the landed, southern elite. Southern honor was rooted in an inner conviction of one's own self-worth and pride about one's morality, values, and unimpeachable conscience; those feelings are projected outward and confirmed by society. In other words, honor began with self. According to the late historian Bertram Wyatt-Brown, "Honor serves as ethical mediator between the individual and the community by which he is assessed and in which he also must locate himself in relation to others." In short, a man was honorable only if his community believed him to be and he had a reputation for being so. Gaines imagined himself honorable and projected that to his Richwood community, which, in turn, accepted him as a man of honor.[23] Honor was not solely determined by character, though; it could also be earned in southern society through wealth—specifically land and slave ownership. The community automatically bestowed honor on a man with Gaines's wealth. Hence, his wealth cemented his standing as an honorable man in his community.

In the Old South, gentility was a higher, more refined form of honor based on the graces of sociability, learning, and piety—although the weight of each of those graces varied depending on location. Sociability is likability, or a person's social graces, disposition, and friendliness. A premium was placed on the spoken word as a component of honor, especially eloquence, charisma, engaging conversation, humor, charm, and wit. Archibald K. Gaines possessed none of the refinement, sophistication, or charisma that would qualify him as genteel. He received only a basic education. He was rather reticent, inarticulate, and generally uncomfortable speaking publicly. What social graces he lacked, he made up for in piety. An active member of Trinity Episcopal Church in Covington, his community considered him "orthodox," and he was known to be supportive of the local clergy.[24]

Physical appearance also mattered among Southern gentility. Gaines was described as a slender man who was slightly above medium height, with a wrinkled face. He had a small head with bushy, gray hair, matched by a gray mustache and goatee. One reporter noticed his "small foot and hand: the latter looks rough, but more from exposure than labor." Gaines's clothing seemed "careless" to the reporter. In the South, physical appearance and stature were considered outward reflections of honor—primal honor. Poor health, a small head or stature, and signs of physical labor such as worn hands could negate or diminish honor. Although Gaines appeared to dress carelessly and had small feet and hands with rough skin, the reporter ultimately assessed that his "general manner and appearance

[were] rather gentlemanly. . . . There is nothing coarse, disagreeable or re-pulsive about his appearance, but on the contrary he seems to be (and we have no doubt he is) an agreeable and intelligent gentleman."[25] "Gentle-manly" men exuded honor, practiced chivalry, and behaved courteously. But "gentlemanly" and gentility are not the same concepts. Gaines would have fallen short of the membership standards of Southern gentility be-cause of his messy appearance, small head, weathered hands, and lack of education, refinement, sophistication, and sociability.

Gaines also seems to have struggled as a slave master in the beginning. Within one year of purchasing Maplewood and its enslaved workforce from his brother John Pollard, Archibald was ready to throw in the towel. His brother Abner, writing to John Pollard reported that Archibald was in "poor spirits" and "determined to sell all the negroes he bought of you." One of John Pollard's sons offered to purchase the slaves from his uncle, but his offer was declined. Archibald said he wished to reserve John's right to reclaim them, should he desire.[26] At the time, Archibald K. Gaines clearly was having some unspecified trouble, but his problems did not seem to be financial in nature. Certainly, if they had been financial, he would have accepted his nephew's offer to buy his bondspeople, hired them out, or sold them down the river. More likely, his enslaved people were being difficult or refusing to submit to his authority. That seems to be the most logical deduction—especially given John P. Gaines's extended absence during the Mexican War and his subsequent service in the legis-lature, during which time his bondspeople may have had loose or lenient management. If so, this might have caused them to resist a more authori-tarian or strict management style.

Whatever his difficulties in 1851, Archibald K. Gaines never sold his slaves. In 1856, he was forty-eight years old; also living at the Maplewood farm then were his pregnant thirty-four-year-old second wife, eleven-year-old daughter, and eighty-two-year-old mother—all named Elizabeth—his ten-year-old son, John, four-year-old daughter, Margaret, and son Wil-liam, who was nearly two years old.[27]

THE MARSHALL FAMILY

James Marshall, a native Virginian, owned a 124-acre farm about a half mile east of Maplewood. His farm was significantly less substantial than his neighbor's, in size, production, and worth. In 1850, he owned six horses, six milch cows, forty sheep, eight cattle, and seventy swine. His farm produced 300 pounds of butter, grew 200 bushels of oats, and 100 bushels each of wheat and flax in 1850. Like other Boone County farmers, Marshall raised hogs to sell. His other money crop was tobacco: in 1850, he grew 800 pounds of it.[28]

Thirteen bondsmen and women worked the Marshall farm in various capacities in 1850. They were a young group—the oldest was a forty-year-old male. Many of the thirteen likely worked cultivating tobacco or raising hogs, since those were his two commercial ventures. He sold his hogs and extra produce in markets in Cincinnati and Covington. Marshall also leased his slaves to others on a temporary basis to make extra money in what was termed a "hiring-out" system. To "hire one's time" or "hire out" meant that bondsmen and women (mostly men were given this privilege in Kentucky, though) were permitted to secure a work contract for wages elsewhere. They could choose their own masters; so naturally, bondspersons would choose masters who treated them humanely and offered good wages. "Hires," as they were called, paid their owners a portion of their wages but were free to keep the rest. Their work terms might be only a few days, but they typically lasted fifty weeks.[29] This arrangement afforded the opportunity for enslaved people to function—more or less—as free people: they chose their employers, negotiated their own contracts and wages like free people, moved about relatively freely, earned wages, and had disposable income. Most used that money effectively and purchased their own freedom and/or the freedom of loved ones; others—especially those hired out in cities, squandered it on vices. Still, this work arrangement gave many enslaved people a taste of freedom—a taste they would not easily forget. Hiring one's time slowly weakened ties to slavery; it made one anxious for freedom and increasingly discontent with one's enslaved status.

With so much at stake, why would slaveholders hire out their slaves? Most resorted to this practice because of financial insecurity. First, the slaveholder could profit from surplus slaves and could bring in additional income when needed. Second, owners did not need to provide food, clothing, or medical care for those hired out to others; that was the responsibility of those who hired them. Finally, owners also could escape taxes during the time their bondsmen and women were hired out to others.[30]

James Marshall routinely and repeatedly rented out his slaves—mostly to people who lived in the towns along the southern banks of the Ohio River.[31] Marshall's habitual participation in this hiring-out system says a great deal about his financial instability—especially compared to Gaines, who did not rent out his slaves. The more owners used this system, the more they destabilized the lives, marriages, and families of their slaves. Enslaved families owned by Marshall were broken up—not because he sold some of them "down the river," but because he hired them out *up* the river—the Ohio River.

At the time of the escape, the Marshall household consisted of the fifty-two-year-old patriarch, James Marshall, his forty-six-year-old wife, Julian, and their five children—including nineteen-year-old Thomas Marshall and a three-year-old girl with a different surname who may have been a niece.

THE GARNER FAMILY

Mary and the elder Simon Garner embody the trauma and destruction of black marriages and families under slavery—even in a state where people boasted about a milder form of it. Both owned by Marshall, the Garners were fortunate enough to have found each other on the same farm. The record is silent about whether the couple chose one another as mates or if they were mated by their owner. It was not uncommon for owners to simply pick mates for their bondsmen and women though.

Although Simon and Mary married, their union was not formal, official, or recognized by the state, and may not even have included a church ceremony or officiating minister. Slave marriages were neither legitimized or recognized by the state, nor respected by slaveholders or white society in general. Even if their marriages had been recognized or respected, enslaved persons could not realistically expect to be able to honor their marital vows and obligations even if they wished—especially the vows about protection, provision, and loving and cherishing one another until death. These unions could be dissolved by escape, when owners sold or hired out either partner to a distant place, or at the whim of the owner. Nonetheless, African Americans still valued marriage and considered it honorable and legitimate. African American marriages were not defined by legal standing, but were built on love plus a mutual decision to be each other's life partners and raise children together. For enslaved couples, marriage proved to be "an act of soul preservation"—an effective way to mitigate the traumas of slavery. Although slavery denied black men the right to be recognized as heads of their families, their wives honored them as such in spirit and practice: sometimes seemingly small gestures affirmed that. For the Garner women, such gestures included taking their husbands' surname.[32]

Motherhood was as painful as it was joyous for enslaved African American women like Mary Garner. Slave codes dictated that the status of a child followed the status of its mother. By the antebellum era—long after the end of white indentured servitude—all children born to white women were free. By contrast, most children born to African American women had no such claims to freedom upon birth, since most African American women were enslaved. In a sense, then, children inherited slavery and freedom through their mother's wombs. Ironically, despite living in a patriarchal society, the father's status did not affect the child's legal status: even if a powerful white man fathered the children, as long as the mother was enslaved, so too were her children—unless, of course, he legally freed them. Regardless of an enslaved woman's own desires, "The rules of slavery governed [her womb,] her fertility, her fate as a mother, and the fate of her child."[33] Pregnant enslaved women carried their children not only knowing that they would be born enslaved, but that they likely would never enjoy freedom and could even be sold away from them. Those stark realizations surely had a deadening effect on whatever joy they might have gotten from an impending birth.

Mary Garner, described by the press as a "very largely built woman" who looked like she possessed "Herculean strength," gave birth to eight children, most of whom had been sold.[34] Hence, in addition to tobacco and hogs, James Marshall also made money by selling and hiring out Mary Garner's children. He treated her as little more than a womb that produced wealth.[35] Marshall clearly did not value Mary's identity as a woman, mother, and wife with a family that she loved as much as he loved his own.

In addition to the trauma of being separated from most of their children, Mary and Simon Garner also endured a lengthy separation from each other. Around 1831, Marshall sold Simon, then in the prime of his life, to George Anderson of Clark County, Kentucky, which was about ninety miles southeast of Richwood. Presumably, this decision was purely financial, because Marshall promised Simon that he would buy him back when he was able.[36] To Simon and Mary—people without the means or permission to travel or the ability to write letters—that ninety miles might as well have been ten thousand. Marshall did not—or could not—honor his word to repurchase Simon for nearly twenty-five years. When he finally did in spring 1855 and brought the elder Simon back to Richwood, the estranged couple promptly rekindled their relationship and Mary reclaimed his surname—proudly later reclaiming her identity as "Mary *Garner*" (she had been using Mary Marshall). This reclamation of her husband, their marriage, and his last name is evidence of the staying power of their love and a testament to the strength of their marital bonds, despite the damage caused by slavery and the extensive separation they endured.[37]

Simon Jr. or "young" Simon Garner—as he was called—born in 1828, was just a few years old when his father vanished from his life.[38] With his father gone for most of his life, he grew up in what effectively was a single-parent family, which were quite common in slavery. Hence, he not only grew up experiencing loss (of his siblings and father) himself, but witnessing his mother agonize about her multiple losses—a pain that must have had a numbing effect on her spirit. The compounded effect of decades of abuse, grief, and loss likely incapacitated Mary to the point that she was incapable of intervening to stop the deadly assault on her grandchildren that fated day. Young Simon would have witnessed his mother's abuse at Marshall's hand. As he grew into his manhood without a father, he likely would have grown more protective of his aging mother.

Peggy Garner was born in slavery on 4 June 1833, in Richwood, Kentucky, also to enslaved parents. Her mother was named "Cilla," or "Cilly" and the identity of her father is historically unknowable. Cilla and Peggy initially belonged to John Pollard Gaines.[39] Cilla resided at Maplewood until being sold for unknown reasons to Gaines's brother, James, in the 1840s. James Gaines owned a huge farm in the area that rivaled plantations in the Deep South in the size of its enslaved workforce and value. Apparently, though, Cilla had given James enough concern that she might run away that he sought to "purchase the negro girl daughter [Peggy] of your [John Pollard Gaines] negro woman to prevent her [Cilla] from leaving the country." James Gaines may have reasoned that if he bought Peggy from John Pollard, Cilla would settle down and not try to escape.[40] This evidence is important for two reasons. First, it demonstrates that Peggy had a propensity to run away—perhaps even a history of it. Second, it suggests that children were at the center of enslaved mothers' decisions to flee bondage. Historians have argued that children were the reason enslaved mothers chose not to flee, but they also heavily factored into the reasons mothers ran away.

Peggy's father may have lived at Maplewood or somewhere nearby at some point.[41] We get only a faint image of him through a historical record that generally ignores the African American fathers of children born into slavery. Enslaved mothers are not particularly visible in the record either.

More than likely, Peggy's father died, was sold, or escaped slavery at some point in her childhood, because he fades from the record and her life. White slave owners from Richwood, though, claimed that he was a man with a "very bad character" and a "revengeful and devilish temper."[42] When men of the slaveholding class used such characterizations about enslaved people, it usually meant they had a history of resistance or possessed a will that refused to be subjugated or broken. Hence, it seems that both of Peggy's parents were rebellious and defiant. One cannot overlook that she inherited a legacy of resistance when trying to make sense of why she broke the chains of slavery that January evening in 1856.

Very little is known about Peggy's childhood other than that when she was only five or six years old, she looked after, or "nursed," Mary Gaines, the daughter of John Pollard and his wife, Eliza.[43] This would have been her primary responsibility then. As Peggy grew up, she would have borne a growing share of household and farm duties at Maplewood. She knew her biological family and grew up in proximity to cousins, aunts, and uncles. Considering the fate of other enslaved people in that era, Peggy is rather fortunate to have grown up with her family and extended family, for at least part of her childhood.

Peggy and Simon Jr. had known each other their entire lives. Simon Jr. was five feet eight and a half inches in height and described as having a "black complexion." The younger Peggy was, according to one account, "a beautiful woman, chestnut colored, with good features and wonderful eyes."[44] When the two married, she was just a teen, and he a young adult. Like Simon's parents', their marriage was not a legal union recognized by the state.

Owned by different families, the young couple did not live together in matrimony under one roof. Instead, they had an "abroad" slave marriage, which is defined as a marriage between two people living in separate places. Abroad relationships and marriages were quite common in places like Boone County where most owners owned only a few slaves, thus decreasing the likelihood of their finding mates at home on the same farm. Although white Kentuckians commonly entered endogamous marriages with relatives, African Americans tended to be exogamous, refusing to marry relatives. Selecting an abroad mate ensured they would not marry within their own bloodline. Owners supported abroad unions for those without viable partners at home; it was in their best interest that their slaves marry so that they could reproduce and increase their slave population and, subsequently, their wealth.[45]

There were multiple disadvantages to interfarm marriages for enslaved couples, but the worst was that they had little power over when and how often they would see one another; owners controlled that. Some owners were more supportive of interfarm marriages and generously allowed family visitation time, whereas others were inflexible and allowed no time away from the farm for such purposes during the week and rarely on the weekends. If one or both owners were taskmasters, then visits to one's spouse were few and far between. In short, slaves' marital obligations were secondary to the needs and whims of their owners. Some enslaved people had to steal away to see their loved ones late in the evenings, on weekends, or during Whitsuntide or Christmas. Given all of these obstacles, most abroad couples could not expect to see each other more than once or twice a week. For Simon Jr. and Peggy, work obligations were a huge impediment to their ability to see each other frequently and bond as a family. Heavy work obligations at Maplewood likely kept Peggy contained and immobile; and Marshall routinely hired his bondsmen out to others who removed them to work in other parts of the state. Both Simon Jr. and his father, for example, had been sent to work for extended periods in other Kentucky communities. The younger Simon had had at least two significant long-term working engagements—one lasting eight months—in Covington, Kentucky, for two different men.[46]

Peggy and Simon Jr. first became parents in 1850 when Peggy was just seventeen and he twenty-two years old. She was perpetually pregnant from then until their escape six years later. It is difficult to know the exact birthdays of the Garner children because slave owners generally kept poor records of the births, deaths, and sales of those they considered property. The Gaineses were no different. Young Simon and Peggy's eldest child, Thomas, called Tommy or Tom, was born in 1850. Samuel, or Sammy, was born in 1852. Little Mary was born 16 August 1853, and Cilla in April 1855. At the time of the escape the Garner children were almost six, four, two years, and nine months. One newspaper report described the boys as "bright-eyed, woolly-headed, cunning looking little fellows, as almost all little black boys are. Their fat cheeks dimple when they laugh." Little Mary was described as "almost white—and was a little girl of rare beauty." Cilla was described as much lighter in color than her mother—"light enough to show a red tinge in [her] cheeks."[47]

When enslaved married people were owned by different owners, as Peggy and young Simon were, their children belonged to the mother's owner. Hence, Archibald K. Gaines directly benefited from Peggy's frequent childbirths. Each child added considerable value to his workforce and, consequently, his wealth. President Thomas Jefferson believed that a slave woman who gave birth every two years was more profitable than the strongest man. He elaborated on that point, "What she produces is capital; while his labors disappear in mere consumption."[48] Jefferson's words affirm, in no uncertain terms, the high valued placed on enslaved women of childbearing years. By escaping slavery, and with all four of her children in tow plus the one in her womb, Peggy literally stole nearly half of Gaines's workforce, plus a portion of his current and future wealth. It is no wonder that he pursued her with dogged determination on 27 January.

Despite their enslavement, the Garners defined and cherished family the same way whites did, although slavery made it difficult for them to practice those values in the same way. Despite living on different farms and being owned by different families, the Garners were remarkably close as a family unit. Through marriage and motherhood Peggy gained a nuclear family and an extended family with a surrogate mother. She had a deep affection for Simon's mother, referring to her as "mother," and Mary, in turn, considered Peggy a daughter. The Garners named their children after their relatives, much like the Gaineses did. In African American families, daughters were often named after their grandmothers, and the firstborn sons often received the name of the father or grandfather.[49] Little Mary and Cilla were both named after their grandmothers, and Thomas may have been named after Peggy's biological father or even Thomas Marshall. That is where the similarities between these families end. All parties understood that the needs and wishes of the Garners would always be secondary to those of the white families who owned them; and this grim reality influenced how the Garners functioned as a family.

Slavery despoiled motherhood for enslaved women and diminished their freedom to practice nineteenth-century maternal ideals. For example, although Peggy may have aspired to be an attentive and nurturing mother, her reality as an enslaved mother on a small farm meant she had little time to either attend to or dote on her children. She was able to keep her children relatively close as she worked, so she could quickly tend to their needs or offer them affection; but hers was no ideal motherhood. Her husband and in-laws lived on another farm, so Peggy bore the burden of raising the children practically by herself. She solely tended to their daily emotional and material needs. Four young children—all under the age of six, needed to be fed, bathed, clothed, kept warm, supervised, and protected from danger. They also needed to be loved, nurtured, socialized, and spiritually fed. All of those mothering responsibilities were compounded by housekeeping in her own living quarters, farmwork, and on-demand duties to the Gaines family: Peggy was nearly perpetually in service to others most of her young life.[50]

Peggy constructed an alternate definition of motherhood that flew in the face of the patriarchal slave society in which she lived and gave birth. She wanted her children to have freedom and all the things associated with that. Her ideals and goals about motherhood centered on her ability to successfully liberate her children. In her mind, a good mother was one who could do that effectively.

After the murder, Peggy defiantly asserted that she—not Gaines—had ultimate authority over her children. Although slave law held that Gaines owned her children and, by extension, her womb and every child born out of it, Peggy rejected that premise and boldly claimed her essential motherhood rights. She believed her children were hers, given to her by God. As their mother, Peggy believed she had the right to choose slavery or freedom, or life or death for them.[51]

Although denied the opportunity to be the kind of mother and wife she might have wished to be, Peggy may have been able to practice sisterhood with the four other enslaved women living at Maplewood. Of the four other enslaved women at Maplewood, three were within three or four years of Peggy's age. Their day-to-day lives at Maplewood are unknowable. These women are more historically invisible than Peggy, because they did not commit an act that catapulted them into the annals of history. One can surmise that these women would have forged a bond of assistance, cooperation, interdependence, support, and sisterhood. While they did not always get along, the group of women may have mitigated the damaging emotional effects of slavery for one another. At the least, having a community of women certainly eased Garner's workload: she would have shared the washing, cooking, spinning, weaving, sewing, quilting, housecleaning, and farming obligations with these other women. During her pregnancies, Peggy likely relied on these women for midwifery and help with her children and chores. Other enslaved women on a farm would have served as an emotional and spiritual sustaining force for her. After all, they could empathize with one another about common abuse and encourage one another not to internalize the effects of it. Moreover, it is possible that these women even collaborated on resistance. For example, one or all of these women may have known that Peggy was planning to escape and may have helped her prepare her children for the journey the evening of the escape.[52] This small group of female peers at Maplewood is the closest thing to a bona fide slave community Peggy had outside of her family. Besides family and community, she may have also found solace in Christianity. There is a small possibility that she was a baptized member of the Richwood Presbyterian Church, since an enslaved woman named Margaret was listed in its records.[53]

Just as surely as slavery despoiled black womanhood, it did the same to black manhood for the Simons. Most men in nineteenth-century America, regardless of race, strived to exercise a patriarchal version of manhood that included authority over their wives and children, providing sustenance, clothing, and shelter, and protecting their kin from threats and danger. Men who did those things effectively gained a sense of self-respect and dignity; those who excelled at them might even develop a degree of pride. Slave owners practiced a concerted and deliberate effort to emasculate black men—slave and free—and render them impotent. As historian Edward Baptist explained, "The denial of black manhood was central to white manhood."[54] Although some individual African American men formulated nuanced definitions of manhood, slavery denied them the opportunity to practice the basic ideals of manhood. As an enslaved man, Simon Jr. could not exercise patriarchal authority over his wife and children: he had to yield that authority to Archibald K. Gaines. Moreover, the responsibility of providing food, clothing, and shelter for his wife and children also belonged to Gaines. So, instead, he must have agonized over the fact that another man filled that role, diminishing his sense of self-respect and dignity as a man. Years later he stated that he escaped because he "wished to exercise his rights and privileges as a husband."[55]

Slaveholders denied black men the fruits of their own labor and the opportunity to provide for their families. Denying black men manhood made slaveholders feel even more powerful. Moreover, husbands could be sold to distant places, away from their wives and children. Enslaved men were powerless to protect their mothers, daughters, sisters, aunts, and friends from physical and sexual abuse at the hands of white men, or any assault or insult by whites in general. Moreover, they could not level grievances or exact vengeance against those who committed these acts.

DRIVEN TOWARD MADNESS

They could only fantasize about heroically defending their loved ones, because acting on it could lead to sale, brutal beatings, or death. Witnessing, seeing evidence of, or having knowledge of the abuse of loved ones and being powerless to protect them, traumatized black men and eroded their self-esteem. Certainly, enslavement was a humiliating and demoralizing condition that was a kind of death for African American men.[56] Conscientious and sensitive black women hoped to minimize such damage. For example, Mary Garner later admitted that she wished her husband had never returned to the Marshall farm after his twenty-five-year absence so that he would not have to witness her abuse.[57] In short, we should not discount how slavery damaged enslaved men as well.

Slavery also undermined men's practice of fatherhood. In young Simon's case, both his abroad marriage and subjugation to the hiring-out system negatively affected his practice of fatherhood. Living on a different farm meant that he could not be present in his children's daily lives and that obstacle was exacerbated by frequently being hired away from Richwood. Around the same time that Peggy was pregnant with their first child, James Marshall hired out the expecting father to James Poor from Covington, Kentucky. Hence, in one instance, the newly formed family was ripped apart. Young Simon's absence likely stressed Peggy beyond reason, especially since her own in-laws had been separated for nearly three decades. Young Simon was away at least eight months then and might have remained gone for an indeterminate and prolonged time period like his father had Poor not unexpectedly passed away, which brought young Simon back to Richwood. Marshall hired him out again soon thereafter. He left again around 1852 to spend an unrecorded length of time in the employ of William Timberlake of Covington. The limitations of interfarm marriages compounded by the frequency of his hires meant that young Simon was an infrequent visitor to his wife and children at Maplewood. The best clue of the infrequency of his visits is that the Garner children seemed to have no idea who their father was, or even what a father was. When asked his father's name after their capture, Tommy reportedly responded, "Haven't got any!" When asked who made him, Tommy's response was, "Nobody!" Certainly the boy's words illustrate that an abroad marriage also lent itself to "abroad fatherhood," which sometimes rendered enslaved fathers virtual strangers to their own children. Limited opportunities to see their children regularly did not mean that enslaved fathers like young Simon had any diminishment of love or affection for them. Despite how slavery inhibited their full expression of fatherhood, these men still treasured it because it gave them a sense of love, purpose, and responsibility. Through fatherhood, enslaved men might exercise a measure of power, authority, and guidance over their children.[58]

Despite these daunting obstacles to traditional practices of fatherhood and manhood for enslaved men, Simon Jr. crafted alternative practices of them. First of all, although blood paternity is the primary basis of fatherhood—the reason most men become emotionally attached to children—for young Simon, fatherhood seemed neither to be determined by biology nor differentiated by it. He must have wondered, like everyone else, whether he was the biological father of some of Peggy's children—especially the girls, who were nearly white in complexion. Despite what must have been gnawing doubts, young Simon sought freedom and safety for them all, regardless.

Young Simon's decision to lead his family out of bondage may have been driven by a concern over the welfare and physical and emotion safety of one family member or the entire family unit. As a husband, father, and adult son, he assumed responsibility for all three generations of Garners. He made it his responsibility to protect all of them. The only real power he had to protect one or all of the Garners was to remove them from bondage. In essence, then, young Simon's ushering his family to freedom can be considered a form of protection. Fleeing was the last hope for a man who could not physically protect his family from abuse and violence. A successful escape with his entire family, then, would restore some of the manhood and dignity that slavery had stripped from him.[59]

Escaping allowed young Simon to exercise not only a protective manhood, but also manly leadership through his thoughtful planning. He was the genius, motivator, organizer, and leader behind the entire escape plan; he put the plan in motion, worked out all of the details related to the escape, including making contacts and arrangements on the other side of the river, coordinating efforts to leave, and securing transportation. Geographical knowledge of how to navigate to a free state was a kind of "freedom capital" for enslaved people. Simon Jr.'s geographical knowledge of northern Kentucky also was an exercise of manhood, because it empowered him, inspired self-confidence, and demonstrated to his family that he was capable of guiding them to freedom.[60]

Although family support networks did much to help enslaved people cope with abuse and various traumas, having an intact family also had some drawbacks. Personal pain and abuse is ultimately absorbed by other family members and loved ones. Enslaved people not only endured their own personal injuries but also were damaged by witnessing the mistreatment of their spouses, parents, children, and grandchildren and being powerless to stop it. Thus, personal trauma for the Garners was also familial and generational and, consequently, compounded and inescapable. It is not surprising that the Garners decided to leave as a family unit: the only way to preserve their entire family unit was to leave together. Their abuse had bound them together, and so would their destinies.

We may never know exactly why the Garners escaped. There may have been multiple reasons for their escape, including the heavy, exacting, nearly incessant work they performed as slaves. The elder Garners had given their best years working to benefit others. Then in their fifties, they could no longer handle the physical demands. The work was enough. They had had enough.

Another huge possibility that led them to flee was all manner of abuse. There may have been a precipitating abusive event, or perhaps their psyches buckled under the compounded stress of their collective grievances and traumas and they decided they could no longer endure it. The abuse was enough. They had had enough.

Another possibility is that the Garners may have feared being sold, and escaping was the only way to keep the family intact. Their history demonstrates that the threats of being sold or separated were constant. For Peggy and the children, there was a looming possibility of being sold down the river, given Archibald's ties to Arkansas. For the Marshall slaves, being hired out and sold up the river was just as much as possibility. Fear of separation and family destruction was enough. They had had enough.

Uncertainties, too, could have pushed them to flee—the uncertainties of not knowing when they would be abused, or how; the uncertainties of not knowing if they would live out their days together in peace, or sold away; uncertainties about their children's future and uncertainties about the paternity of all children born to women in bondage. Uncertainty was enough.

Finally, there is the possibility that the escape was born of opportunity and the desire for freedom. Simon Jr. recently had gone to Cincinnati and met with his wife's family there and thus was able to plan an escape.

Because it was a very cold winter, he knew the river would be frozen and could be crossed on foot. It is possible that the family had talked for years of escaping, but now with contacts in Cincinnati, and the frozen river to facilitate the crossing, the moment to act on their collective desire for freedom was at hand. And so they headed to the Promised Land, as a unit. The Promised Land north of slavery beckoned them, just as the multiple fears and horrors of slavery pushed them to leave.

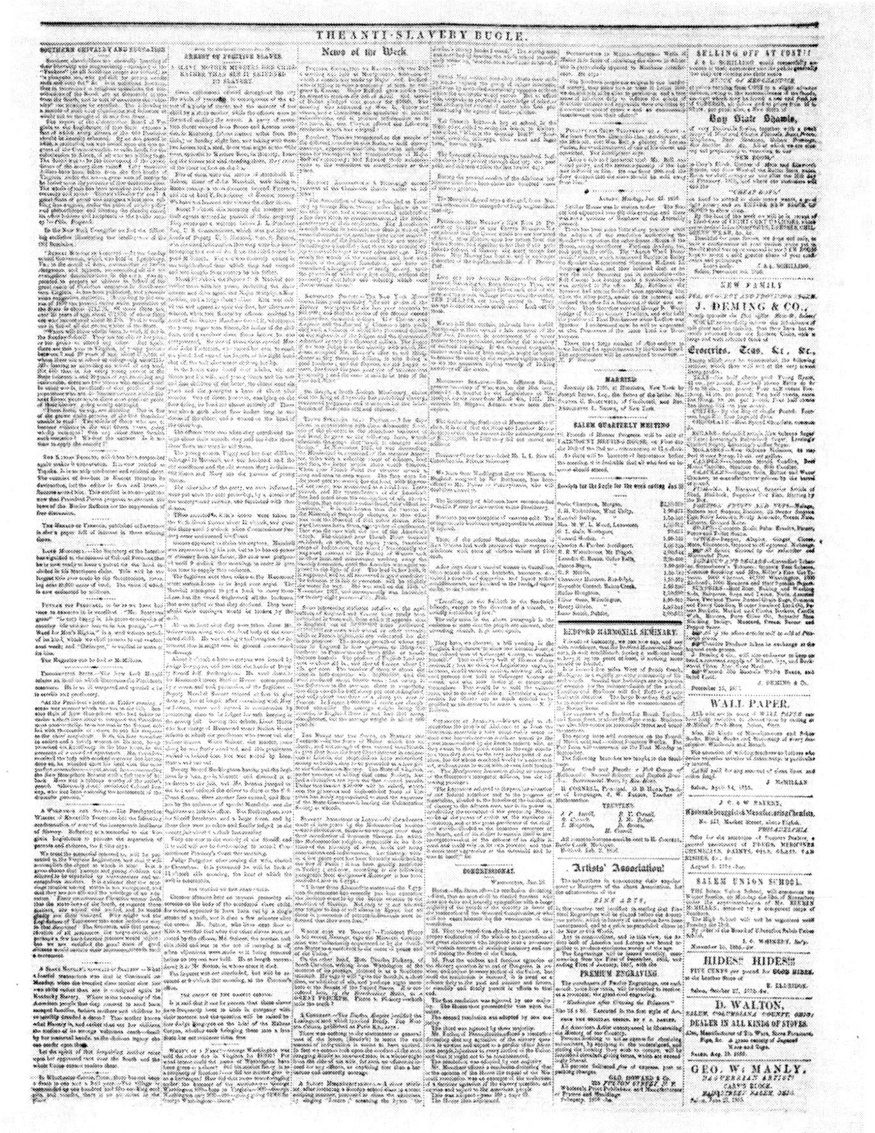

THE ANTI-SLAVERY BUGLE.

News of the Week.

J. DEMING & CO.,

WALL PAPER.

HIDES!! HIDES!!

D. WALTON,

GEO. W. MANLY,

Plate 1. *Anti-slavery Bugle*, 2 February 1856. Image 3. Library of Congress

Plate 2. Murder indictment for the Garners, 8 February 1856. Courtesy of the Ohio History Connection. State Archives Series 631

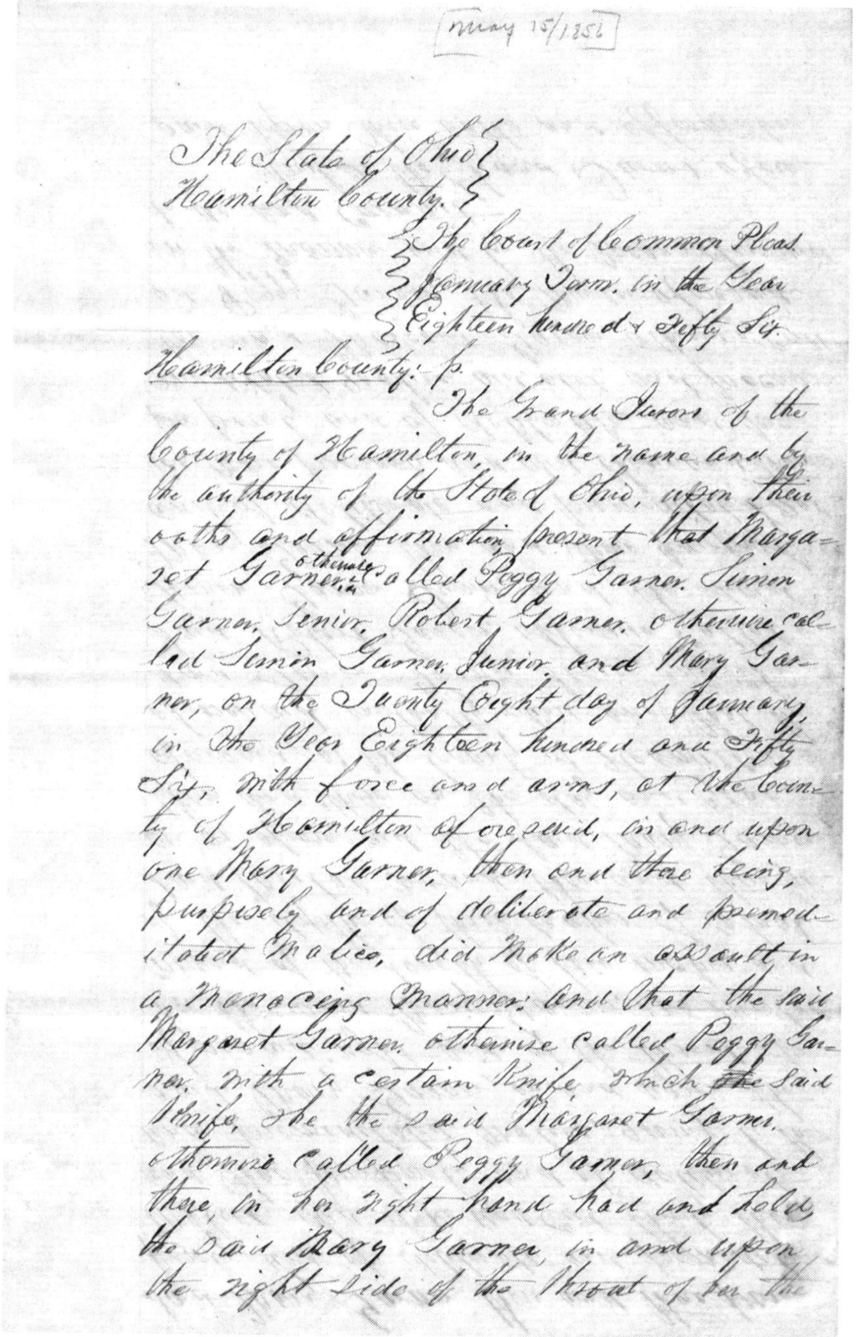

The State of Ohio
Hamilton County.

> The Court of Common Pleas
> January Term, in the Year
> Eighteen hundred & Fifty Six

Hamilton County: ss.

The Grand Jurors of the County of Hamilton, in the name and by the authority of the State of Ohio, upon their oaths and affirmation present that Margaret Garner otherwise called Peggy Garner, Simon Garner, Senior, Robert Garner, otherwise called Simon Garner, Junior, and Mary Garner, on the Twenty Eight day of January, in the Year Eighteen hundred and Fifty Six, with force and arms, at the County of Hamilton aforesaid, in and upon one Mary Garner, then and there being, purposely and of deliberate and premeditated Malice, did make an assault in a Menaceing Manner; and that the said Margaret Garner, otherwise called Peggy Garner, with a certain Knife which the said Knife, she the said Margaret Garner, otherwise called Peggy Garner, then and there, in her right hand had and held the said Mary Garner, in and upon the right side of the throat of her the

---

Plates 3a–c. Hamilton County prosecuting attorney Joseph Cox's narrative of the Ohio murder indictment against the Garners, 15 May 1856. Courtesy of the Ohio History Connection. State Archives Series 631

said Mary Garner, then and there purposely and of deliberate and premeditated
Malice, did strike and Cut Wisely then
and there purposely and of deliberate
and premeditated Malice, giving to the
said Mary Garner, in and upon the
aforesaid right side of the throat of
her the said Mary Garner, one Mortal
wound of the length of five inches and
of the depth of three inches of which
said Mortal wound, then and there given as aforesaid, the said Mary Garner,
then and there, on the day and year
aforesaid, at the County of Hamilton
aforesaid instantly died and that the
said Simon Garner, Senior, and the
said Robert Garner, otherwise Called
Simon Garner Junior, and the said
Mary Garner then and there purposely
and of deliberate and premeditated Malice were present, and did then and there
purposely and of deliberate and premeditated Malice, aid, abet, and procure
the said Margaret Garner, otherwise Called Peggy Garner, the Murder aforesaid
in the Manner and by the Means aforesaid
to do and Commit.

And the Grand Jurors aforesaid upon their oaths and affirmation

aforesaid, do say that the said Margaret Garner, otherwise called Peggy Garner, the said Simon Garner, senior, and the said Robert Garner, otherwise called Simon Garner, junior, and the said Mary Garner, the said Mary Garner then and there on the day and year aforesaid, at the County of Hamilton aforesaid purposely and of deliberate and premeditated malice did kill and murder, contrary to the form of the Statute in such case made and provided, and against the peace and dignity of the State of Ohio.

Joseph Cox
Prosecuting Attorney,
Hamilton County, Ohio

The State of Ohio
Hamilton County ⟩ sct.

I, Thomas Spooner Clerk of the Court of Common Pleas within & for the County aforesaid do hereby certify that the foregoing is a true copy of the original Indictment on file in said Court in the case therein stated.

Witness my hand & the seal of said Court this 15th day of May A.D. 1856.
Thomas Spooner Clerk
By E. P. Cranch Deputy

Copy of Order to Sheriff

United States of America.
Southern District of Ohio

In the matter of Simon Garner
Simon Garner Jr Mary
Garner and a negro
woman named Peggy otherwise
called Margaret Garner

The Sheriff of Hamilton
County having brought the parties above named before
me on the habeas corpus heretofore issued together
with the cause of their detention by him. The
Court upon full investigation find that said
parties were in the custody of the United States
Marshall for the Southern District of Ohio
and were unlawfully taken from such custody
by said Sheriff and are now unlawfully detained
by said Sheriff and the Sheriff after the
hearing of this cause applied for leave
to amend his return by setting up proceedings
occurring since said hearing which the Court find
to be irregular and disallowed. It is therefore
ordered that said Sheriff deliver said parties
into the hands of said Marshall to be disposed
of according to law.
In testimony whereof I Humphrey H Leavitt
Judge of the District Court of the United States
for the Southern District of Ohio before whom
this proceeding herein were had. have hereunto
set my hand and Seal this 28th day of
February A.D. 1856
(signed)   H. H. Leavitt
(Seal)

Plate 4. The order given to the sheriff to deliver the Garners to the federal marshal, 28 February 1856. Courtesy of the Ohio History Connection. State Archives Series 631

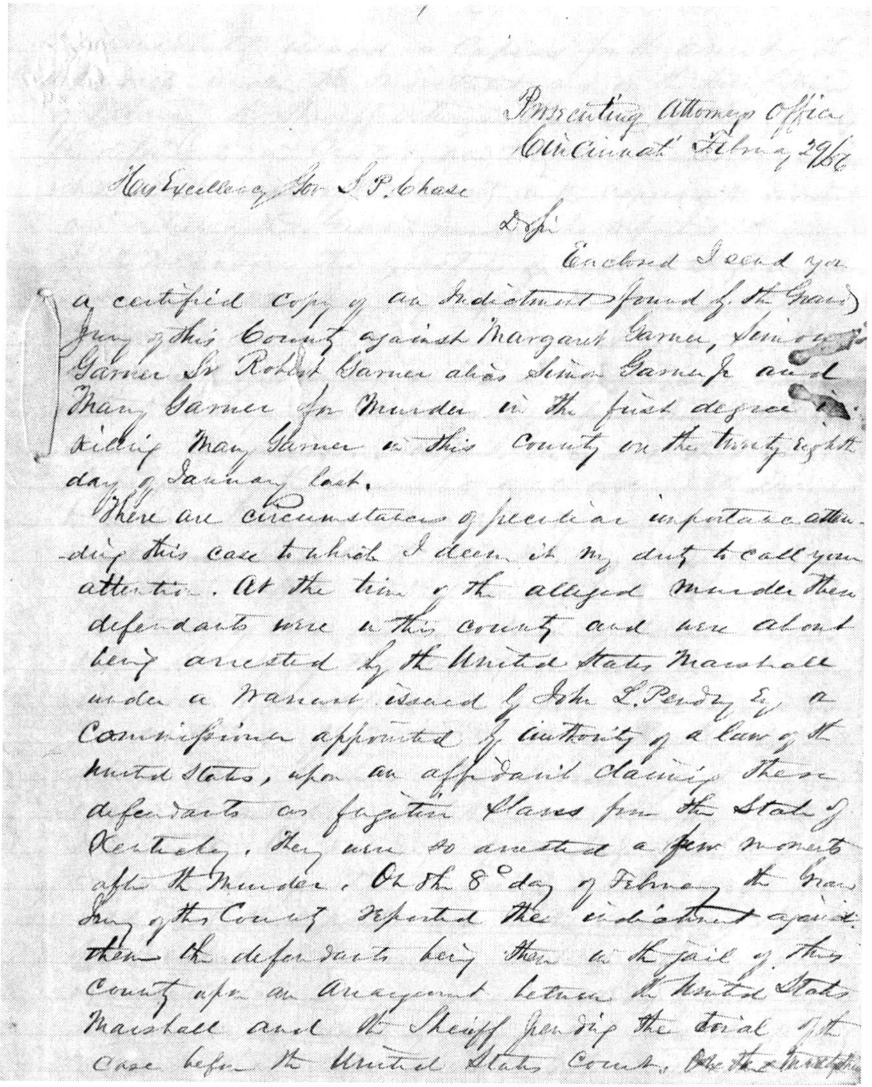
Prosecuting Attorneys Office
Cincinnati Febry 29/56

His Excellency Gov S. P. Chase

Dr Sir

Enclosed I send you a certified copy of an Indictment found by the Grand Jury of this County against Margaret Garner, Simon Garner Sr Robert Garner alias Simon Garner Jr and Mary Garner for Murder in the first degree in killing Mary Garner in this County on the twenty eighth day of January last.

There are circumstances of peculiar importance attending this case to which I deem it my duty to call your attention. At the time of the alleged murder these defendants were in this county and were about being arrested by the United States Marshall under a Warrant issued by John L. Pendery Esq a Commissioner appointed by authority of a law of the United States, upon an affidavit claiming these defendants as fugitive Slaves from the State of Kentucky. They were so arrested a few moments after the Murder. On the 8th day of February the Grand Jury of this County reported the indictment against them the defendants being then in the jail of this County upon an Arrangement between the United States Marshall and the Sheriff pending the trial of the case before the United States Court. On the [illegible]

Plates 5a–d. Letter from county prosecutor Joseph Cox to Governor Salmon Portland Chase, 29 February 1856, outlining the state and federal custody battle over the Garners. Courtesy of the Ohio History Connection. State Archives Series 631

I immediately issued a Capias for the arrest of the defendants under the Indictment and on the twenty third of February the Sheriff returned the Capias that he had the defendants in Custody and they were accordingly served while in the jail of this County with copies of the Indictment and a list of the Grand Jurors who reported the same. In the meantime the question under the Fugitive Slave act was still pending before the United States Commissioner and was not decided until the twenty sixth of February when the Commissioner without having the defendants before him, they being during the decision in jail, decided that they were the property of the Claimants and ordered the Marshall to deliver them into their custody.

On the 25 of February Judge Leavitt of the United States District Court for the Southern District of Ohio issued a Writ of Habeas Corpus to the Sheriff of this County, requiring him to produce the bodies of the defendants before him and also his authority for detaining them. The Sheriff made return that he held them by virtue of the Capias aforesaid and appended to the same a copy of the Indictment. On yesterday Feby 28 Judge Leavitt proceeded to decide the question on said Habeas Corpus and held that said parties were in the Custody of the United States Marshall for the Southern District of Ohio and were unlawfully taken from such custody by said Sheriff and are now unlawfully detained by said Sheriff, and ordered that said Sheriff deliver said parties into

the hands of said Marshall to be disposed of according
to law". A copy of said order is hereto appended.
Upon this order all of said defendants were immediately
on yesterday delivered one at the jail of this County by
the Sheriff into the hands of the United States Marshal
and by him immediately removed into the State of
Kentucky beyond the jurisdiction of this State.)

I cannot make any affidavit or ~~with~~ our statement
that these parties are fugitives from justice in order
to ask a requisition upon the Governor of Kentucky
for them. They did not flee from justice in this
State but were taken out of the State by the
overwhelming force of the United States Marshal
and his posse.

I have laid the facts before you for such action
as you deem advisable. The highest crime known
to our law has been committed upon the territory
of this State, and the authorities of the State are prevented
from vindicating the law and protecting the lives and
property of her citizens, upon the ground that the perpetrators of the crime "owe service and labor" to the citizen
of another state. If this be so, the citizens of this
State hold their lives and property at the mercy
of neighboring Slave States, whose slaves may cross
the line burn and destroy our property and take our
lives and then the whole force of the United States
Government be brought to tear the perpetrators from

from the authority that would punish them under
our laws, simply because they were slaves.

This State ought to see, that every crime
committed on her soil shall be punished
according to law, and it is the duty of the General
Government to protect the Sovereignty of each
individual State against any mere claim of
private property. If you deem it proper to
issue a requisition upon the Governor of Kentucky,
for these defendants, I leave it with you to select
such agent as you may see proper to receive
them on behalf of this State from the authority
of Kentucky —

Truly yours,
Joseph Cox

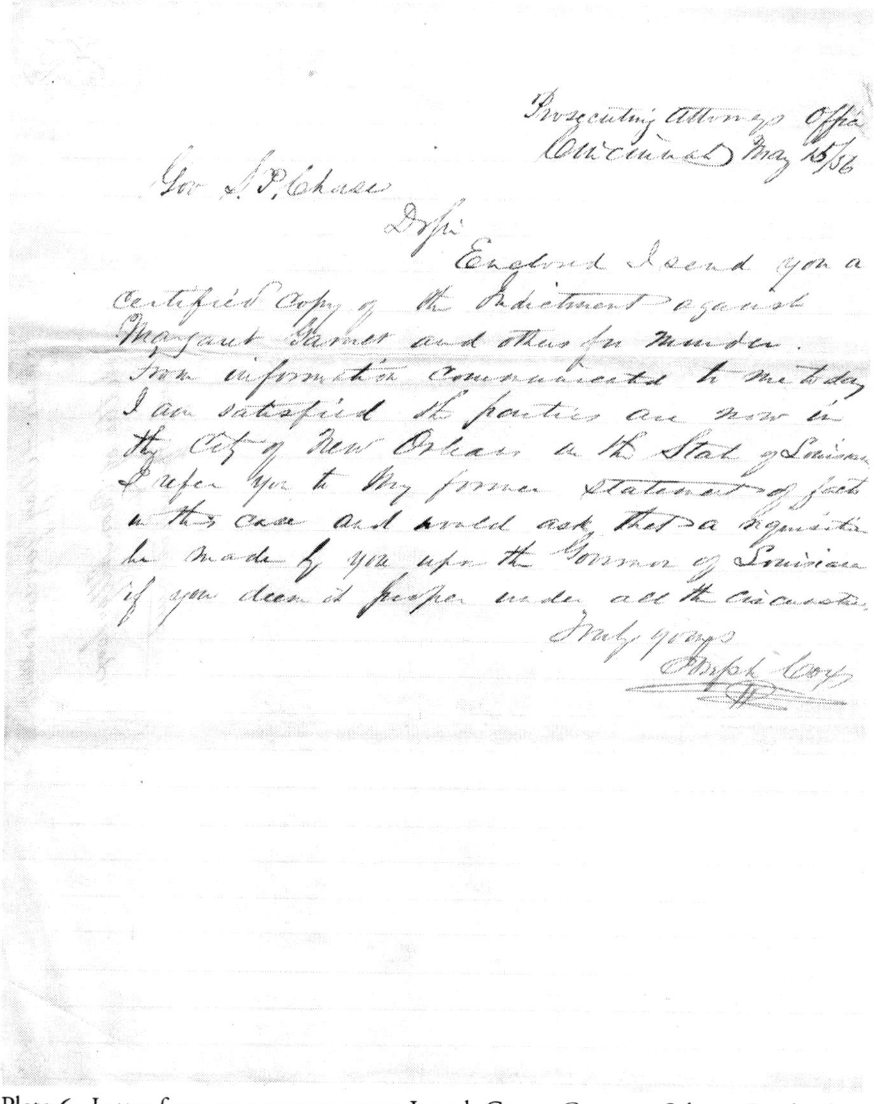

Prosecuting Attorney's Office
Cincinnati May 15 /56

Gov. S.P. Chase

Dr Sir

    Enclosed I send you a certified copy of the Indictment against Margaret Garner and others for murder. From information communicated to me today, I am satisfied the parties are now in the City of New Orleans in the State of Louisiana. I refer you to my former statement of facts in this case and would ask that a requisition be made by you upon the Governor of Louisiana if you deem it proper under all the circumstances.

    Truly yours
    Joseph Cox

Plate 6. Letter from county prosecutor Joseph Cox to Governer Salmon Portland Chase, 15 May 1856. Courtesy of the Ohio History Connection. State Archives Series 631

3

AFTER THE BLOOD

Thus, did a Roman Father slay,
The idol of his soul,
To screen her from a tyrant's lust,
A tyrant's foul control.

Though this was done, in days of yore
The act was truly brave;
What value, pray, is life to man,
If that man be a slave?

Go and ask of Margaret Garner,
Who's now in prison bound,
(No braver woman e'vr hath trod,
Columbia's slave-cursed ground).

Why did she with a mother's hand,
Deprive her child of breath!
She'll tell you, with a Roman's smile,
That slavery's worse than death.

—James M. Bell, 1856[1]

If the Garners had to be captured, Cincinnati was the best possible place for it: they could not have dreamed of a more organized and aggressive abolitionist community determined to resist their return to slavery than the one in Cincinnati, Ohio. This community had a robust and long history of assisting fugitive slaves dating back to the first few decades of the nineteenth century. By 1840, there was a large, dedicated network of families who regularly provided shelter, food, and transportation for fugitive slaves. African American families who regularly provided assistance to runaways in Cincinnati included Thomas and Jane ("Aunt Jane") Dorum, who were widely known throughout the free black community in Cincinnati and the slave communities of northern Kentucky; William Casey and his son; and John and Francis Hatfield and their daughter Sarah. Other African American conductors included the Hall and Burgess families, who hid fugitive slaves in their homes on McAllister Street and Longworth Street, respectively. William Watson, one of the city's more successful barbers, and Henry Boyd, a wealthy corded bedstead manufacturer, also harbored fugitives from time to time. Cincinnati had an active vigilance committee, which was a team of abolitionists committed to assisting fugitive slaves through a range of activities like traveling to Kentucky to meet with prospective fugitives, coordinating the points and times of their departures, rowing them cross the river, escorting them from the river to places of refuge in the city or onward to more northern and western locations, hiding them in their homes, and providing disguises, food, medical care, and extra clothing.[2]

White abolitionists also harbored and forwarded fugitive slaves in the city. Local abolitionist editors and attorneys James Birney and Gamaliel Bailey, as well as Salmon Portland Chase, abolitionist attorney, governor of Ohio, and future Supreme Court justice—all harbored slaves in the 1830s.[3] Birney had been arrested, tried, and convicted of harboring a fugitive slave in 1837, although the case was eventually overturned by the Ohio Supreme Court. Another operative was Levi Coffin, who by the 1840s became one of the most effective of the city's white operatives. In an 1893 letter, President Rutherford B. Hayes reveals an Underground Railroad network that included Cincinnati's most powerful men, including himself, a justice of the peace, county prosecutor Joseph Cox, and police court attorney William Dickson.[4]

This community not only had a committed and effective interracial community of Underground Railroad conductors, but also boasted abolitionist ministers, editors, journalists, teachers, novelists, feminists, attorneys, and judges. These activists had spent their resources, reputations, and careers battling slavery. For example, Harriet Beecher Stowe, author of the best-selling antislavery novel *Uncle Tom's Cabin*, published in 1852, lived in Cincinnati for years. Abolitionist editor James G. Birney and abolitionist attorney Salmon Portland Chase cut their abolitionist teeth in Cincinnati before going on to build national reputations and careers for themselves as powerful antislavery advocates and a Supreme Court justice. Abolitionist teachers like Augustus Wattles and Peter H. Clark dedicated their careers to educating freed slaves and using the classroom as a powerful breeding ground to raise the consciousness about slavery. Few abolitionist communities utilized as many abolitionist practices as Cincinnati.

Although a northern city with a dedicated, organized, and diverse abolitionist community, Cincinnati was not an antislavery city, by any means. Proslavery support abounded, and abolitionists actually were a minority—a committed and active minority, but a minority, nonetheless. Proslavery support dominated in this northern city situated in a free state, in part because the city's economy was heavily dependent on its commercial relationship with the slave South. The city's primary economic endeavors—steamboat manufacturing and pork packing—thrived because of trade with the South. Cincinnati merchants, manufacturers, and nearby farmers produced crops, goods, and foodstuffs that slaveholders purchased to support their enslaved workforce. Northern Kentucky farmers like Gaines and Marshall raised hogs for the Cincinnati pork-packing industry. The steamboats manufactured in Cincinnati transported goods and passengers to southern ports. Throughout the decades preceding the Civil War, Cincinnati's economy waxed and waned depending on whether southerners perceived city business and political leaders as supportive of slavery.[5] To protect those interests and relationships, Cincinnati leaders routinely endorsed the repression of abolitionist activism, even if that repression included mob violence. The city also nurtured virulent populist proslavery and prejudiced sentiments that sometimes lent themselves to antiabolition and antiblack mob violence. The city witnessed three significant mobs in 1829, 1836, and 1841 that effected a forced exodus of half of the city's black population, a reign of racial terrorism, and a race war, respectively. Despite the climate and the persistent threat of mob violence, Cincinnati's abolitionists seemed undeterred. They proved to be no less committed, organized, or fearless than abolitionists in Boston or New York City.

The George Washington McQuerry case is the first that tested southwestern Ohio's abolitionist commitment to resist the 1850 Fugitive Slave Act. In 1849, McQuerry and three others escaped from slavery in

Washington County, Kentucky. While the others wisely continued on to Canada, McQuerry settled in Miami County, Ohio, which is roughly forty miles from Cincinnati. There, he got married, fathered two children, and by all accounts lived for four years as a "sober industrious man, a good husband, a respected neighbor." McQuerry's owner found him sometime in 1853, prompting his arrest and removal to Cincinnati to stand before a US marshal.[6]

When news about McQuerry's arrest circulated in Cincinnati, the black community immediately mobilized to protest his return to slavery. The fact that he had not been a member of the Cincinnati black community was of little concern: his freedom hung in the balance, and that was enough. African American protesters gathered outside the hotel where McQuerry's owner was staying, but the police quickly dispersed the crowd. Meanwhile, Peter H. Clark, black civic leader and trustee of the Colored School Board, applied for a writ of habeas corpus to have the US marshal holding McQuerry show just cause why he had been deprived of his liberty. Had it not been for the quick application for the writ, McQuerry likely would have been carried back to Kentucky without incident.[7]

McQuerry had the advantage of having Cincinnati's best abolitionist attorneys, John Jolliffe and James Birney, working on his behalf to secure his freedom. The attorneys' defense focused on the fact that McQuerry's four-year residence in Ohio granted him de facto freedom. The heart of their defense, though, challenged the constitutionality of the 1850 Fugitive Slave Act. His legal representation reasoned that the denial of the right to a trial made the legislation unconstitutional. The case was brought before Justice John McLean, who sat on the US Supreme Court, but was in Cincinnati at the time attending to his circuit court duties (at this time Supreme Court justices also traveled the circuit and presided over trials and hearings as "circuit justices"). McLean ruled in favor of McQuerry's owner, reasoning that he must uphold the law.[8] Although McQuerry eventually was returned to his owner, no one can discount how the Cincinnati abolitionist community had acted on several levels to try to protect his freedom.

In October 1853, another case tested both the law and the commitment of Cincinnati's abolitionist community. According to Levi Coffin, a slave known simply as Louis escaped from Kentucky and settled in Columbus, where he lived for a number of years until his owner discovered his whereabouts, at which time Louis was arrested under the 1850 Fugitive Slave Act and taken to Cincinnati. Louis's friends telegraphed Cincinnati's abolitionist attorneys, alerting them to the case. This time, defense attorneys challenged the slaveholder's claim to Louis by arguing that he was free because his owner had previously brought him to Ohio. This claim of freedom was granted by the 1841 *Starr v. Farr* dictum, which automatically freed bondspeople who entered the state with their owner's knowledge and consent. On the day the decision was to be rendered Louis decided not to take his chances with the American justice system. He inched his way backward into the crowded courtroom ever so slightly so as not to be noticed by authorities. Those in the crowd, though, noticed he was trying to escape and gave him a series of encouraging nudges and taps and made way for his exit. The crowd slowly parted and quietly made room for Louis to inch his way backward toward the court door. Someone in the crowd even placed a "good hat" on his head to disguise him. Soon, Louis was outside the courthouse. A few minutes passed before the court noticed he had escaped, but by then he was aboard the Underground Railroad and on his way out of the city.[9]

Finally, the 1855 Rosetta Armstead case tested the limits of Ohio as a state that protected black freedom. For decades, abolitionists and Underground Railroad agents had been informing enslaved people who came to the city with their owners' permission that Ohio laws made them free. That included those who stopped in the city with their owners while in transit to other places, those sent into Cincinnati to do errands, or those permitted to attend church service or visit relatives.[10] The Rosetta Armstead case centered on the freedom of Rosetta, a Louisville bondswoman. While on a steamboat journey to Wheeling, Virginia (now West Virginia) with her owner's agent, Rosetta and her party were unable to continue due to ice on the Ohio River. The agent decided to continue the trip by train, so he took her from the steamboat into the city of Cincinnati to catch the train. By doing so, he unwittingly subjected Rosetta to two forces which undermined her bondage: Ohio's laws, which outlawed slavery and a very conscientious abolitionist legal community. She was legally freed. The Rosetta case proved that it was very risky for slaveholders to stop in Ohio with servants in tow, even if momentarily.[11] All of these previous cases came to inform the Margaret Garner case.

The Garners were taken from the Kite residence to the US courthouse around noon on 28 January 1856, and held there until Commissioner John

L. Pendery convened court at 3:00 p.m. Gaines claimed Margaret and her children as his slaves; and Thomas Marshall attempted to claim the older Garner couple and Robert. But Marshall did not have a proper power of attorney to act on behalf of his ill father, so Pendery postponed court proceedings until 9:00 the following morning in order to give him time to return to Richwood to get it. In the meantime, federal marshals moved the fugitives to the Hammond Street jail for safekeeping overnight.[12]

Coroner John Menzies began investigating Mary's death that same day. In the coroner's inquest, routine in murder cases then, the coroner acted as a detective and conducted an initial investigation about the cause and method of death and determined who was responsible. Menzies focused on discovering who killed Mary, because that answer was not immediately obvious to anyone besides those who had been inside the Kite home. He interviewed all of the Garner adults, who were initially reticent. Margaret lied about her role, implying that the child was killed in the melee during their capture. Because people standing outside the Kite residence had seen Elijah's wife open the back door and send her son to dispose of the bloody knife in the privy, Menzies initially believed she had killed the child. On the morning of 29 January, the coroner summoned a jury of six men and called several witnesses to answer his questions about the toddler's death. Chief among those witnesses were the Garners and the Kites. In this inquest, the Garners made their initial claim of cruelty and abuse as the reason they had escaped. Mary Garner made it clear that they never conspired to kill the children should they be threatened with capture, and that to the best of her knowledge, Margaret had not premeditated the act. After their brief testimony, the coroner's jury deliberated and quickly reached a verdict that same day, finding that little Mary Garner had been murdered by her own mother with a butcher knife. Interestingly, too, the jury concluded that Robert and Simon had been accessories to the murder. Mary Garner is the only Garner adult not implicated in the child's death by this jury—largely based on her own testimony that she hid under a bed during the murder.[13]

While the Garners were in the custody of the US marshal, George S. Bennett, and lodged at the local jail, abolitionists secured a writ of habeas corpus from the probate court judge John Burgoyne on 29 January. Judge Burgoyne instructed Deputy Sheriff Jeffrey Buckingham to bring the prisoners and their captor (the US marshal) before him to explain why they were being held. Sheriff Gazoway Brashears and his assistants went to the jail to deliver the writ to the local police and marshal holding the family. Police lieutenants argued with the sheriff, refusing either to recognize the legal authority of the writ or even allow him to see the Garners. The police lieutenants claimed that the fugitives had been placed in their charge by Marshal Bennett and refused to relinquish them except on his orders. Sheriff Brashears and his party threatened to force their way into the cells to retrieve the Garners. Meanwhile, Menzies's investigation triggered the process for a murder warrant for the Garners, which was not served because the family was in federal custody.[14]

The confusion ultimately centered on who had jurisdictional authority over the Garners, the state or the federal government. As fugitive slaves, the Garners fell under the jurisdictional authority of the US marshal and his deputies and were subjected to the 1850 Fugitive Slave Act; as suspects in a murder, they came under the jurisdiction of the State of Ohio and sheriffs. The former suspended the writ of habeas corpus, and the latter allowed it as a way to safeguard people's right to a fair trial. The police lieutenants at the Hammond Street Station believed that the federal marshals had jurisdictional authority, so they initially refused to turn the Garners over to the sheriff under the state's writ.[15] The questions of which charges should be answered, state or federal, as well as who had jurisdictional authority over the Garners would dog this case until the end.

Once Marshal Bennett and his deputies arrived at the police station, they and the police agreed to move the prisoners to the US courthouse. A large crowd followed them as the federal marshals moved the family. Sympathizers shouted to the Garners to "stand by their freedom" and encouraged them not to give up. Perhaps inspired by fugitive slave Louis's escape from federal marshals, the crowd pleaded with the deputy sheriffs to rescue the Garners. Guns were drawn by police and marshals, on one side, and county sheriff deputies, on the other. A federal marshal vowed to shoot down anyone who would "lay violent hands on the prisoners" in order to wrest them from the "officers of the Confederacy." Cooler heads prevailed, and officials agreed that the Garners should be returned to jail until the hearings began the next morning.[16]

The proceedings of one of the most dramatic, divisive, sensational, and emotional cases ever heard under the Fugitive Slave Act of 1850 began at 9:30 the morning of 30 January 1856, before Commissioner John L. Pendery. Proceedings were covered in the local press.[17] Cincinnatians took great interest in the case. Each day throngs of sympathetic onlookers and abolitionists protested outside the courthouse. Unfortunately, Marshal Bennett barred African Americans from courtroom. A crowd—composed of two to three hundred African Americans and a "few prominent whites of a certain political stamp"—a euphemism for abolitionists—protested the Garners return to slavery, demanded entry into the courtroom, and even tried to block the movements of the family as it moved to and from the courthouse. African American women were the most vocal and active voices of protest in the crowd. The proslavery, racist, Democratic newspaper, the *Cincinnati Daily Enquirer*, claimed that these women, dressed in "the extreme of fashion," viciously cursed and verbally assaulted the police officers. In response to an officer's orders that they stand back, one woman reportedly said, "D—n you! D—n you, I'm free born, half white, and as good as any white-livered b—h in Ohio!" The *Daily Times* reported that the black women "cursed most disgustingly" at the jailers.[18] Although the newspapers intended to cast these female protesters in a negative light, the reports reveal the passion and tenor behind their protests. This case was a huge touchstone for them because they would have personally identified with Margaret's dilemma as an enslaved mother seeking freedom for her children; they would have felt personally vested in the family's fate. Their protests are significant because they are the first documented collective and public protests by black women on behalf of another black woman in US history.

Pendery decided to split the case in two, with James Marshall's claim on Robert and his parents' being heard first. John W. Finnell and S. T. Moore served as attorneys for James Marshall, and Colonel Francis T. Chambers served as counsel for Gaines. John Jolliffe, one of Cincinnati's leading abolitionist attorneys, represented the Garners. Introduced to antislavery principles by his Quaker upbringing, Jolliffe had been involved in antislavery activities for decades. He had served as an officer in local branches of the American Anti-Slavery Society and had been a delegate at antislavery conventions. As an attorney, Jolliffe had taken on fugitive slave cases without pay for decades.[19] For example, he had represented Joseph Kite when Wilson Harper sued him for breach of contract for failing to follow through on the agreement to purchase Elijah's freedom, as discussed earlier. Jolliffe was one of three Cincinnati attorneys blessed with both eloquence and persuasive litigation skills, who also were committed to abolition, knew Ohio's case law related to slavery, and had experience fighting for fugitive slaves' freedom. The Garners were in extremely capable hands with Jolliffe representing them.

Jolliffe chose a legal strategy that focused on securing the Garners' freedom by arguing that their owners had willingly brought them into Ohio on previous occasions, therefore entitling them to their freedom. Black freedom had been secured in Ohio's foundational documents. Not only did the 1787 Northwest Ordinance prohibit slavery in the territory that would later become the state of Ohio, but after the state was founded, its constitution (1803) also prohibited slavery and involuntary servitude. In 1841 an Ohio circuit court ruled in *State v. Farr* that a party of slaves who had been brought into the state by their owner who was on his way to Missouri were free by virtue of having been freely brought into a free state by their owner. The circuit court justices in that case had rejected the principle of comity—or the idea that slave owners' property rights were protected as they traveled through free states with their slaves. The justices reasoned, "Bringing slaves into this state with the view of passing through it to settle in another state made such persons free."[20] This analysis shaped the abolitionist logic that served as the basis of the Garners' defense. The logic held that Margaret Garner was legally free based on the fact that she had been brought to Ohio previously by her owner.

Despite having skilled counsel, the Garners had federal law working to tighten their shackles. The 1850 Fugitive Slave Act denied fugitive slaves due process, including the rights to trial by jury and habeas corpus. Instead, fugitive slave cases were to be held in front of commissioners. Compounding those legal disabilities, section 6 of the 1850 Fugitive Slave Act provided that "in no trial or hearing under this act shall the testimony of such alleged fugitive slaves be admitted into evidence." Because the law denied fugitives the right to even testify on their own behalf at their hearings, the cards were stacked in the slave owners' favor. Jolliffe was forced to, instead, secure affidavits as proxies for the Garners' testimony. In these affidavits, Mary, Robert, and Margaret all swore that they had been taken or sent to Cincinnati previously by their owners—Robert as recently as December, Mary five years before, and Margaret when she was a child. It all seems likely because in border towns like Cincinnati, it was commonplace for slave owners to send or bring their slaves into the city for a variety of reasons, including for conducting business. Unable to read or write, all three signed their names on the affidavit with simple "Xs." Because the point of the affidavits was simply to prove prior visits to Cincinnati, as historical evidence they offer little insight into much else about the Garners' lives in bondage.[21]

Next, Jolliffe made a motion asking that Commissioner Pendery allow the fugitives to be served the state warrant for murder. His strategy was to get the Garners brought under Ohio juridical authority, instead of federal jurisdictional authority, which leaned in favor of their owners. Pendery quickly decided that the state warrant for murder would not be served until after both fugitive slave cases had been presented and resolved.[22]

Never one to resist an opportunity to fight for racial equality, Jolliffe then spent some time challenging the court about racial discrimination. Cincinnati's black community had been complaining, agitating, and organizing about Marshal Bennett's decision to exclude them from the courtroom as spectators. Black activists printed and distributed handbills that read "Geo. S. Bennett, U.S. Deputy. Let the public mark this man, and let the nation fear for his safety when LECHEROUS DRUNKEN TYRANTS are in power." The handbill closed with "The people of Ohio send Sharp's rifles to Kansas, yet permit their own soil to be invaded by bullying Kentuckians, sided by their dog BENNETT."[23] In addition to passing out these handbills, African Americans noisily and vociferously protested their exclusion outside the courthouse by throwing rocks and cursing at officers. According to one report, an African American man with a knife in hand approached the mayor outside the courthouse and managed to grab him by the throat before being restrained.[24] They clearly were passionate about this case. Believing that African Americans had a right to witness the proceedings, on 31 January Jolliffe asked Commissioner Pendery in open court if he had issued an order excluding them from the courtroom. Pendery denied that he had issued such an order, but added that if they indeed had been excluded, it had been done by Marshal Bennett and without his consent or authorization. Jolliffe complained to the commissioner that since African Americans had not been allowed into the courtroom, he would be forced to "hunt up" witnesses himself. He then asked the court why Marshal Bennett had served witness subpoenas for the slave owners but not the Garners. Bennett responded by explaining that the 1850 Fugitive Slave Act did not mandate that he serve subpoenas on behalf of the fugitive slaves' witnesses, so he refused to do so. To remedy that procedural loophole, Jolliffe requested that Commissioner Pendery appoint a special deputy marshal to serve subpoenas to African American witnesses and recommended William Beckley, a well-known and respected biracial man, for the job. When Gaines's attorney, Colonel Chambers, objected, Jolliffe responded that Beckley was "a citizen of Ohio, and a voter," underscoring that he was more than respectable enough to represent the court. Pendery allowed Beckley to serve the subpoenas to black witnesses. Beckley's appointment is remarkable because it is, perhaps, the first time in the history of the United States that an African American served as an officer of the court—and a federal court, at that. African Americans were finally allowed into the courtroom as witnesses on 1 February and as spectators five days later.[25]

Jolliffe next focused on challenging the arrest warrants on two technicalities. The first is that the arrest warrant for Robert had been issued in the wrong name—Simon—and was, therefore, invalid. The second technicality was that the warrant did not have a proper state seal as mandated by law.[26] Jolliffe's claim about Robert's legitimate name simply was not true. Everyone—including their own kin, knew the couple only as Peggy and Simon Jr.—not their freedom names Margaret and Robert.[27] Moreover, because they were enslaved, they did not have legal names recognized by the state anyway, so Jolliffe's claim on the names was inconsequential. Further, the debate over the seal, as Pendery retorted, also was inconsequential. To his credit, Jolliffe did try every angle he could to invalidate the legal claims of Gaines and Marshall. The hearing proceeded.

Marshall's attorney called on witnesses from Boone County who affirmed that the two Simons and Mary Garner all belonged to him. Some of the witnesses, including Thomas Marshall, testified that they never had seen or known of the Garners to have ever been in Ohio. However, Thomas lied several times in his testimony, including denying ever taking Robert into Cincinnati the previous Christmas—despite conflicting facts about that trip and a half dozen witnesses to the contrary.[28]

After Marshall's attorney rested his case, Jolliffe began calling witnesses—mostly African Americans—on 1 February. African Americans had only received the right to testify against whites in Ohio courts in 1849. Jolliffe deliberately called only the most respectable witnesses who belonged to black civic and religious organizations. These witnesses recalled, with amazing detail, instances when they previously had seen various members of the Garner family in Cincinnati. The Garner witnesses included all of the Kites and some whites who previously had done business with Marshall. They all affirmed that Robert Garner had accompanied his owner on business many times. The witnesses also corroborated Robert's claim that he had been in the city with Thomas during the Christmas season.[29]

In his closing argument on behalf of his client, J. W. Finnell tried to undermine Jolliffe's central argument that the Garners had been to Ohio previously and were, therefore, free. Finnell insisted that the federal laws recognized and protected slavery. The main thrust of his closing argument used the decision in the Supreme Court Case, *Strader et al. v. Graham* (1850). That suit was brought by a slave owner (Graham), against the owner of a steamship (Strader), because Strader's ship had carried three of Graham's slaves from Louisville to Ohio without his permission; once there, they fled to Canada. Strader's defense focused on the fact that the slaves were musicians who had been given permission by their owners to make the journey multiple times before. The Kentucky courts ruled in favor of Graham, stating that Strader did indeed contribute to the loss of those slaves by allowing them onto his ship without their owner's permission, and was ordered to pay damages. Strader filed an appeal that focused on proving that Graham often allowed his slaves to cross into the free states of Ohio and Indiana previously; and by doing so, they were legally free according to the Northwest Ordinance long before they got on his ship. Strader lost again, so he appealed to the US Supreme Court, which unanimously held that, except as limited by the Fugitive Slave Clause of the US Constitution (Article IV, Section II, Clause 3) and the federal laws on that issue, a state could decide for itself who was enslaved or free. The high court also held that the Northwest Ordinance was no longer applicable because the US Constitution superseded it. Such a decision made slavery more secure by holding those who helped facilitate an escape financially accountable to the slave owners.[30]

The premise of Jolliffe's closing argument on behalf of Robert Garner and his parents is that the Garners were humans—fathers, mothers, and infants—who deserved freedom. He used several strategies, including invoking Christianity, the theory of Natural Rights, and moral suasion. He believed that the Fugitive Slave Act and Christianity were morally exclusive. "The law of '50 (The Fugitive Slave Law) commands you to treat those people as slaves; the Bible as men. . . . Don't you see that the Bible is on one side and the Fugitive Slave law on the other?" Jolliffe's own abolitionist sympathies could not be contained in his speech; and at times, he demonized the slave owners. Underlining the difference between the black and white Kentuckians in the room, he thundered: "The only difference between them is that while they [looking at the Garners] are basically struggling for freedom, that man [looking at Thomas Marshall] comes into Court, his hands all dripping with warm blood, and asks to take the father of that murdered infant back into interminable slavery and the grandfather into everlasting bondage." Jolliffe also used a bit of hyperbole to emphasize his point when he railed, "Slavery is cannibalism, not that of eating, but of selling human flesh and blood, one cuts the man up for food, and the other sells him for money. Now, sir, are you required to dip your hands in this bloody system of Cannibalism." He finished by imploring the court, "Take your pound of flesh, but not one drop of blood." In other words, he urged the court to punish the Garners instead of sending them back to slavery in Kentucky. In his rebuttal, Chambers insisted that Jolliffe's charge that Marshall had come into the court "with hands dripping with warm blood" was an injustice to the man. Marshall, he insisted, was not answerable for Mary's blood. Chambers ended his statement by implying that Jolliffe was a fanatic. The Marshall case closed on 7 February 1856.[31]

Meanwhile, the state moved ahead with its case. On 7 February, a grand jury indicted Margaret and the other Garner adults for Mary's murder. This indictment prompted yet another federal-state struggle over jurisdictional authority over the Garners, a struggle that went on for two more days. Sheriff Gazoway Brashears seized physical custody of the Garners that same day and refused to take them to the conclusion of their fugitive slave hearing. He eventually agreed to take them before Pendery to allow the fugitive slave hearings to reach their conclusions. The following day, Commissioner Pendery ruled that although the sheriff would retain physical custody, the federal marshals would retain legal jurisdiction until the end of the fugitive slave hearing.[32]

After a two-day intermission to sort through the indictment, custody, and jurisdictional issues, the hearings resumed 9 February. This time, the court heard Archibald K. Gaines's claim on Margaret and her children. An hour into the proceedings, Margaret and her children were brought into the courtroom. A reporter described her in detail. His report is the most thorough physical description of Margaret that exists. He wrote:

> She is about five feet three inches in height, rather stoutly than delicately made. She is mulatto, showing from one-fourth to one-third white blood. Her forehead is high, and has a protuberance (not so large, of course) but something like that which made Daniel Webster's so striking. Her eyebrows are delicate lines finely arched, and her eyes, though not remarkably large, are bright and intelligent. The African appears in the lower part

of her face—in the broad nose and thick lips. Her ear is small; her wrist and hand large.[33]

She wore a dark calico dress, with a small handkerchief on her shoulders pinned close to her neck. Another handkerchief—a yellow one—was wrapped like a turban around her head. A plain gold or brass ring adorned the pinky finger of her left hand—likely a wedding band, albeit on the wrong finger. The reporter also observed two scars on her face, on her left temple and left cheekbone.[34] Margaret's clothing and accessories reflected her sense of style, pride in her appearance, and an air of respectability. The handkerchief around her neck, for example, served as an accessory that added flair to the dress. The handkerchief-style head wrap, itself a distinctive style of enslaved women, served both aesthetic and functional purposes: adornment and protecting the head from the sun and absorbing sweat while working in the fields; such head wraps also proved to be convenient covers for neglected hairstyles. Given the fact that Garner was not working that day, she may have worn the handkerchief head wrap because she did not believe her hair to be presentable enough for court.

Margaret held Cilla in her arms with the "usual tenderness of a mother," while her sons played at her feet. The reporter noted that mother and daughter exchanged loving smiles and Margaret playfully bit at Cilla's fingers with her lips. Despite these moments of maternal love, Margaret's disposition, it was reported, overall reflected "extreme sadness." She may also have been grappling with regret for what she had done. Margaret kept her eyes cast downward the entire time except for an occasional "timid, apprehensive glance" around the courtroom.[35] Margaret's interaction with Cilla and her abiding sadness underscore her humanity: she was a mother who had lost a child, even if at her own hand. Hers would have been a "disenfranchised grief" (grief not publicly acknowledged or socially supported—meaning that people tend not to support grievers who are responsible for the deaths of their loved ones). Because Margaret had murdered her daughter, society assumes she did not possess normal maternal affections for, or attachment to, the child and, therefore, did not mourn her loss.[36] The sadness observed by the reporter suggests otherwise.

For the next few days, multiple witnesses for Gaines testified that Margaret and her children belonged to him. His witnesses included his family physician, Dr. Elijah Smith Clarkson, James Marshall—who had recovered from his illness by then—and other Richwood neighbors and

Maplewood employees. Unable to refute that Gaines owned Margaret and the children, Jolliffe focused on proving that Margaret had been taken to Ohio with John Pollard Gaines and his wife, Eliza, when she was six or seven years old. Apparently, Margaret had accompanied them to help care for their infant daughter, Mary. If Jolliffe could prove that this visit indeed had occurred, then Margaret and her children born after that were also legally free. Jolliffe called five free African American women to the stand to support the fact that slave girls as young as five or six could, and did, serve as nurses for white children. He hoped their testimony would lend some credence to Margaret's claim of having cared for Mary Gaines when she was just a small child herself. None of these witnesses, however, testified that they had seen her in Cincinnati. To strengthen his weak case, Jolliffe called Margaret Garner to the stand on 11 February—not to testify for herself, but as a witness for her children. Although the Fugitive Slave Act precluded testimony by an alleged fugitive, this court allowed it. Consequently, Margaret Garner is the only fugitive slave ever to testify at a hearing under the 1850 Fugitive Slave Act. Commissioner Pendery had allowed her testimony against the stringent objections of Gaines's attorney. Because her testimony was intended to prove that she had been brought to Ohio as a young girl by her previous owner, Jolliffe questioned her only on those facts. His line of interrogation centered on the details of that trip; he asked nothing about the quality of her bondage, life in Richwood, or what had driven her to kill her daughter. Colonel Chambers chose not to cross-examine Margaret, confident that Jolliffe had failed to prove she had been to Ohio. Both sides concluded their cases on 13 February.[37]

TESTIMONY AND TRAUMA

Margaret Garner remains enigmatic, even after at least three history books, multiple historical novels, a play, and a movie, because she said so little while in custody, during her hearing, or afterward. She provided no written account attesting to her experience. Her story is presumed lost or unrecoverable because of the scarcity of words she spoke publicly. If we limit the evidence to traditional historical sources, then perhaps her perspective is lost. When researching black women's history, one must be ingenious and flexible about what constitutes evidence. Garner's truth is not revealed through her direct words alone—written or spoken—but also through insinuations, euphemisms, actions, and even markers on her body. In short, Margaret Garner "testified" to her past trauma in a variety of ways. The murder of one child and attempted murders of her other three children speak volumes about the trauma at the Maplewood farm that had driven her to such desperation.

Garner had other opportunities to testify to her own truth when she spoke to two ministers and a women's rights advocate while in custody and before the hearing. Although the visitors did not know her, they were deeply sympathetic. They each published a summary of their exchanges with Margaret; their collective memories provide some insight into who she was. Still, their accounts are abridged and filtered so much, that they leave more questions than answers. Of the three visitors, Reverend Horace Bushnell, a Congregational minister who previously had been active in the Ohio Anti-Slavery Society, was most direct with her.

> Q: "Margaret why did you kill your child?"
>
> A: "It was my own," she said; "given me of God, to do the best a mother could in its behalf. I *have done the best I could!* I would have done more and better for the rest! I knew it was better for them to go home to God than back to slavery."
>
> Q: "But why did you not trust in God—why not wait and hope?"
>
> A: "I did wait, and then we dared to do, and fled in fear, but in hope:—hope fled—God did not appear to save—*I did the best I could!*"[38]

Although she said little, there is a lot of power in these comments. First, Margaret Garner's retort to Bushnell that her murdered child "was my own" and had been given to her by God suggests that she had defiantly seized her natural maternal authority and prerogative to make decisions about her children—even life-and-death decisions. Her proclamation that her children belonged to her, not Gaines, was itself a type of resistance because it rejected the idea that slave owners had ultimate authority over enslaved children.[39] Second, Margaret's words that "hope fled" and that "God did not appear to save" reveal a deep and abiding sense of despair, hopelessness, and God-forsakenness. In other words, she had tried to embrace a passive form of Christianity that waits for God to save people from their oppression. After her prayers remain unanswered and hope faded, Garner decided to activate bodily salvation herself. Hence, God's failure to rescue her family from bondage had pushed her away from Christianity and toward humanism, with its emphasis on humans' capacity to solve society's problems.

The most telling part of this conversation is her statement that her family had "fled in fear." She gave absolutely no insight into what the family feared; but many who escaped from slavery did so because of rumors of a sale of a child or themselves or other loved ones.[40] The fear of a sale would have been particularly difficult for the Garners, who were a tight-knit family that had lived near one another their entire lives (except the older Simon). A threat that any part of that unit could be separated through sale could have impelled them all to run. After all, the internal slave trade had decimated African American families. One million enslaved people were separated from their loved ones through this trade. A slave child born in 1820 in Kentucky had a 33 percent chance of being sold further south during his or her lifetime, and one third of all marriages were destroyed by this trade.[41] So the fear of a sale of one or several of the Garner family members would have been terrifying. Another type of fear that could have caused them to flee was the fear of physical abuse—or of a particular kind of abuse, perhaps directed at the children.

Still, running away out of fear and murdering one's offspring are two different things. Margaret's conversation with Reverend Bushnell reveals that she had tried several options to save her children from their horrible lot before she resorted to murder and attempted murder. First, she had tried holding onto faith that God would alleviate their situation. When that failed, the family escaped. Killing the children was the last of several hopeless options for a mother who loved her children and wished to protect them. Because Margaret had failed to kill all the children, in her opinion, she had failed to fully liberate them, exclaiming, "I did the best I could!" This statement is loaded with agonizing despair that she had not done enough as a mother to save her children from bondage. Her pained words are a jarring reminder that enslaved mothers like Margaret could not control the quality of their children's lives. More important, they could not secure freedom for them in the here and now no matter what they tried. Her despair also reflects a reality for her that life in bondage was akin to a "perpetually suspended death sentence."[42]

Even after having time to reflect, Margaret still had no regrets about her deeds. Reverend Bushnell claimed that he had tried to awaken in her a sense of Christian remorse or guilt for her sin. He reported that Margaret had "no remorse, no desire of pardon, no reception of Christ or his religion." When he tried to get her to receive Christ, she defiantly told him that she believed Christianity to be a religion of slavery, which was, in her opinion, "more cruel than death." She believed that Christianity had made a compact with slavery, so she wanted no part of either. She refused to allow her soul to be saved by a religion that had never saved her body from slavery. If Margaret Garner ever *had* been a Christian, she no longer professed the faith by then. Reverend Bushnell tried in vain to stimulate her Christian mores. Margaret Garner's only regret was that she had not completed her goal of taking the lives of all four children. Reverend Bassett commented that she seemed to take satisfaction that at least little Mary was "free from all trouble and sorrow."[43]

Reverend P. C. Bassett of Cincinnati's Fairmount Theological Seminary also spoke with Margaret Garner on 29 January while she was in custody. Baby Cilla was in her arms when he entered her cell. Reverend Bassett noticed a large scar on Cilla's head where her mother had hit her with a shovel. He asked Margaret how the baby got the scar, and she bluntly admitted that she had done the deed. Margaret added in a matter-of-fact tone that if she had had more time, she "would have killed them all." Reverend Bassett reported that through tears Margaret had told him "the story of her wrongs" and "days of suffering, of her nights of unmitigated toil." If we take them at face value, these words suggest that her work and torment were nearly perpetual. According to Bassett, Garner's face had the look of pure "agony" as she recounted what life was like for her on Gaines's farm. In other words, her expression and tears confirmed the narrative she relayed. When Reverend Bassett asked if she had been mad when she committed the act, she responded, "No . . . I was as cool as I now am; and would much rather kill them at once, and thus end their sufferings, than have them taken back to slavery, and be murdered by piece-meal." This sentiment speaks volumes about how horrific slavery had been for her: the cumulative effect had murdered her little by little each day. For her, slavery was death—not a quick, final death, but a slow, repetitive, agonizing one. And since freedom had eluded her children on earth, she had decided to secure freedom for them through death. In her mind, death was the only way they would be free.[44]

Margaret Garner's final visitor was Lucy Stone, an abolitionist and women's rights advocate who lived in Cincinnati at the time. Stone had spent the better part of a decade lecturing and lobbying for equal citizenship rights for women and is credited with being the first person to go to the legislature to advocate for those rights. She believed that motherhood, marriage, and especially slavery denied women rights over their

Figure 3.1. Lucy Stone, November 1853. Photograph by G. W. Bartlett. Library of Congress

own bodies. Lucy Stone believed in women's bodily autonomy and had spent the better part of her career fighting to liberate women from various forms of bondage. Just before the Garner trial, she had lobbied on behalf of women's rights within the confines of marriage. She and Henry Black-well publicly denounced marriage for reinforcing legal inequality between women and men before their marriage in May 1855. Stone had insisted on a prenuptial contract that protected her past earnings and outlined that she would maintain financial and personal independence within the marriage, including the right to determine "when, where and how often" she would become a mother.[45] Such radical demands—especially during the Victorian era—made Lucy Stone a pioneer in women's marital rights. When she came to visit Margaret Garner in jail, Stone came as an abolitionist and someone sympathetic to women's rights, specifically bodily autonomy. Unfortunately, despite the myriad biographies of Stone, few even mention her affiliation with Margaret Garner.

After Stone's visit with Margaret, a prison deputy assigned to guard the family reported that Stone had tried to pass Margaret a knife. On hearing these serious allegations, court officials summoned Stone to court to explain her actions. At the adjournment of the hearing on 13 February authorities brought Lucy Stone into the courtroom to respond to the deputy's allegations. Solemnly dressed in a black silk gown, a brown merino wool shawl draped on her shoulders, a matching wool bonnet, and a green veil, Stone mounted the witness stand. She denied ever trying to provide Margaret with a knife. She then took the opportunity to address the audience in an effort to shed light on what had driven Garner to such horror:

> When I came here and saw that poor fugitive, took her toil-hardened hand, and read in her face deep suffering and an ardent longing for freedom, I could not help bid her be of good cheer. I told her that a thousand hearts were aching for her, and they were glad that one child of hers was safe with the angels. Her only reply was a look of deep despair—of anguish such as no word can speak.[46]

Although she glossed over the details of the conversation between the two, like Reverend Bassett Stone claimed to have "read in her face" untold stories of suffering. According to her, Margaret's "eye beamed with the dull light of despair, the tear of anguish trickled down her cheek; her lip quivered in silent agony" as she recounted her story. The *Cincinnati Daily Gazette* reported that Stone went on to level a serious accusation against Gaines and slavery:

> The faded faces of the negro children tell too plainly to what degradation female slaves submit. Rather than give her little daughter to that life, she killed it. If in her deep maternal loves she felt the impulse to send her child back to God, to save it

DRIVEN TOWARD MADNESS

from coming woe, who shall say she had no right to do so? That desire had its root in the deepest and holiest feelings of our nature—implanted alike in black and white by our common Father. With my own teeth would I tear open my veins, and let the earth drink my blood, rather than wear the chains of slavery. How then could I blame her for wishing her child to find freedom with God and the angels, where no chains are?[47]

The reference to "faded faces" implies that Margaret had been raped and impregnated by her rapist; hence, she had been driven to kill her children to save them from a similar fate.[48] Stone believed Margaret's vision of freedom included liberation from bondage, sexual abuse, and the torment of being a mother of enslaved children. She sympathized with Margaret's sentiment that death would be kinder than slavery and admitted that she had casually told the guard that she wished Margaret had a knife to end her misery.

Stone defiantly proclaimed, "I asked no privilege of the Marshal—I beg my rights of none." Then contradicting herself, Stone thundered: "I had a right to put a dagger in the woman's hand—the same right that those had who seized their weapons to fight about a paltry tax on tea. I hoped to see her liberty rendered her—I hope it still." Another newspaper reported Stone's comments differently here, adding: "If she had a right to deliver her child, she had a right to deliver herself. So help me Heaven! I would tear from myself my life with my teeth, before I would be a slave!" Stone believed that God had not intended for anyone to own another: despite Margaret's being enslaved and claimed by Gaines as his property, in her mind she possessed the ultimate ownership of her body and the bodies of her children, including the right to destroy these bodies at will. From this perspective, then, suicide would be an assertion of self-ownership, among other things. Stone continued, "I make no apology to the Court or anyone for wishing to give this woman a dagger. . . . I exercise the same right as those who distributed weapons to the combatants on Bunker Hill." In short, she equated the freedom suicide of an enslaved woman with the American revolutionaries. Stone told the court audience that she also had spoken to Gaines, who promised her to free Margaret Garner as soon as they returned to Kentucky.[49] By inserting herself into the drama of the Garner hearing and defending Margaret in open court, Stone—as a leading figure in the women's rights movement—had placed slave women's experiences in the center of her own campaign for women's freedom and equality.

Margaret's conversations with Bassett, Bushnell, and Stone, coupled with her testimony on the witness stand in her own fugitive slave hearing constitute the only extant testimony of Margaret Garner—the only time she spoke for herself. Unfortunately, these accounts reveal too little of her life before the escape. The silences in Margaret Garner's various oral testimonies leave us wondering what specific horrors she had endured at Maplewood.

Her oblique testimonies are not surprising, especially considering how a straightforward testimony about trauma is not always possible. Traumatic events sometimes can complicate or even prevent the possibility of witness.[50] Testimony about trauma can be incomplete, incoherent, or fragmented because survivors dissemble, forget to remember, dis-remember, deny the truth, hide the truth, and tell half-truths. Even when trauma is divulged, or witnessed, sometimes it "is spoken of only in the moment of testimony; beyond that it is always untold, unspoken, and its truth unknown."[51]

With such obstacles, how can historians recover the history of trauma, verify it, or qualify its intensity when the testimony about it is often fragmented, unspoken, or told through the words and filters of others? Garner's inability to fully and directly reveal her personal trauma in her own words does not mean it did not occur. To prevent the tendency to conclude that silences mean that trauma did not happen, feminist scholar Judith Butler insists that we must not "dismiss the psychic register of pain, nor to read the absence of empirical evidence or narratable history" as a sign that the trauma never occurred. In order to understand trauma, historians must learn to read "what is said silently."[52]

Margaret Garner's body provides clues of what happened to her while she was enslaved. Witnesses noticed that she had two scars on her face: one on her left temple, and the other on her left cheekbone. The flesh embodies people's personal narratives: it is a roadmap to past injuries. Flesh can be a site of historical information and offers a primary source of evidence of the injuries people have endured. Scars can be evidence not only of injuries, but also of abuse. They are the voice of physical pain that attest that physical trauma occurred—even when the survivor refuses to be a corroborating witness to the same. The full story that birthed the scars, though, is knowledge that only the scarred person and the injurer *fully* know.[53] Margaret's flesh bore witness to the truth that she had been beaten and endured some physical abuse while enslaved at Maplewood.

By the late antebellum era, facial scarring on an enslaved person was not as common as it had been in earlier eras. That contemporary witnesses noticed her scars is proof that they were disfiguring.[54]

In the telling and retelling of this story, few people then or now have fully acknowledged those wounds on Margaret's body, the physical abuse that had produced them, or the emotional trauma involved; but they are part of her story and must be acknowledged. When asked how she got her scars, Margaret offered only, "White man struck me."[55] Although she offered no details about the circumstances in which she had been hit, the scars suggest she was struck with an object and with some force, because open-hand slaps do not leave scars. Deep, painful scars to the body and psyche "attempt to tell us of a reality or truth that is not otherwise available." Her scars attest to a level of brutality that she had endured face to face. The broken, "ripped apartness" of Margaret's flesh is evidence of "high crimes against the flesh." As an African American woman, her body became a slate upon which powerful white men could and did inscribe their economic, racial, and sexual power and dominance. The scars underscore how powerless Margaret had been to resist the person who had inscribed his violence and power onto her face. Scars are never simply scars when inflicted by violence; they are disfigurations. Disfiguration is not only evidence of physical trauma but also the material evidence of a wounded spirit.[56] It is rather ironic that Margaret had, herself, also delivered a disfiguring blow to her daughter's face when she hit her with a shovel.

The reading of scars as evidence of a slave's personal history is not unusual. After all, slave traders and buyers considered scars evidence of slaves' histories of rebelliousness or disobedience. Potential buyers "read" the number of and severity of the wounds and scars as a measure of how unruly the person had been in his or her past. They subsequently manufactured histories for the people who stood before them that seemed to, in their minds, correspond with the scars. They also made judgments about the character of those bearing the scars.[57] Bad scarification, they concluded, meant that the person was troublesome, and therefore such people were considered less valuable or even unsalable. Rarely, if ever, did slave dealers or potential buyers read these scars on enslaved people as evidence of the owner's malignity. It is reasonable to conclude, then, that the scars enslaved people bore say as much about the character of the owners as the slave's spirit of resistance.

Sexual abuse is another example of a physical trauma that is endured outwardly and inwardly. Sexual abuse, with all of its brutality, violence, and capacity to traumatize, may explain the impulsive nature of Margaret's actions. Enslaved women who had been raped expressed emotions such as guilt, fear, resentment anger, and rage. At times, prolonged sexual abuse led enslaved women to do unthinkable things to escape it. For example, just six years earlier in Callaway County, Missouri, Celia bludgeoned Robert Newsom's skull, ending his life and years of sexual abuse at his hands. The fact that enslaved women lived in the same households with, worked for, and gave birth to the children of their rapists intensified and prolonged their trauma.[58] We must ponder what it means for a woman to live with and work for her rapist and be subjected to ongoing and inescapable sexual abuse.

As a group, the Garners complained of mental cruelty, inadequate provisions, and physical abuse. According to the *Daily Cleveland Herald*, the family exhibited scars which they said had been inflicted by their owners. Mary Garner, the most forthcoming about the nature of their mistreatment on the Marshall farm, recounted that as she became older, weaker, and less capable of hard work, Marshall had grown more exacting and inhumane in his treatment. She also complained that they were not provided with enough food to sustain them, driving her to steal food in order to keep herself and her husband alive. Although elderly enslaved people did not usually retire, many owners reduced their workloads. This was not the case with Marshall, who clearly aimed to get as much work as he could from Mary. For Marshall, a struggling farmer who could barely provide for his enslaved workforce as it was, Mary represented diminishing returns: she could no longer reproduce and nor was she as physically productive as younger women. The aging woman could no longer physically or mentally tolerate the brutality and cruelty. In her mind, the escape was worth the risk, because the worst thing that could happen to her was death, which she did not fear in the least.[59]

Abuse had broken and wounded Mary Garner's spirit. At no point is that fact more obvious than the day the fugitive family arrived in Cincinnati. Mary, the only other adult in the room when little Mary was being murdered, did nothing to stop Margaret from killing the granddaughter who bore her name. In fact, she responded by running away from the scene and hiding under a bed. Only a wounded spirit and incalculable fear would immobilize someone to the extent that they

DRIVEN TOWARD MADNESS

are unable to defend their own, defenseless grandchild. Reflecting later, Mary Garner emphatically stated that she would have done the same as Margaret under similar circumstances.[60]

An independent witness in the hearing corroborated the Garners' claims about mental cruelty and dehumanization in the hearing. Jacob Rice, a German butcher who had done business with James Marshall a few years earlier, testified that he and Robert had once stayed at his home over-night while doing business in Cincinnati. When Rice and his wife offered Robert a bed too, Marshall strenuously objected, insisting, instead, that he sleep on the bare floor. The butcher asked him why he treated Robert that way and asserted that African Americans are humans just the same as they. Marshall retorted that they were more akin to animals.[61] At the very least, this testimony suggests that Marshall did not believe in African Americans' humanity or equality and treated them as inferiors.

The Garner men were not as forthcoming about the nature of the abuse they suffered, offering no insight into their traumas. They were in custody at least a month before either uttered anything about how they had been treated in Richwood. Their relative reticence is a function of so-cial norms that dictated that men should not complain about abuse. Their reticence in no way suggests that the men suffered less than the women.[62]

The Garners endured all of this abuse individually and collectively. Mary Garner pointed to the emotional damage the men endured watch-ing their female kin being abused and overworked. She explained that despite her boundless joy to see her husband's return to the Marshall farm after twenty-five years, she preferred that he had never come home at all, rather than for them to witness the abuse each endured.[63] If Stone's alle-gations of Margaret's sexual abuse were true, that surely intensified the family's anguish. Such abuse degraded and defiled the victimized women, and emasculated their husbands and fathers. Any devoted and loving hus-band who could not protect his wife and children from abuse could not help but feel inadequate and helpless, if not also enraged.[64] For example, in a different story, Henry Bibb recounted his own feelings of anger and helplessness while witnessing his wife being mistreated by her owner:

> I was compelled to stand and see my wife shamefully scourged
> and abused by her master; and the manner in which this was
> done, was so violently and inhumanly committed upon the
> person of a female, that I despair in finding decent language to

describe the bloody act of cruelty. And unfortunately for me, I am the father of a slave, a word too obnoxious to be spoken by a fugitive slave. It calls fresh to my mind the separation of husband and wife; of stripping tying up and flogging; of tearing children from their parents, an [sic] selling them on the auction block. It calls to mind female virtue trampled under foot with impunity. But oh! When I remember that my daughter, my only child, is still there, destined to share the fate of all these calamities, it is too much to bear. If ever there was any one act of my life while a slave, that I have to lament over, it is that of being a father and a husband of slaves.[65]

After the Garners were apprehended by authorities, Jolliffe said that they told him that they would rather be charged with capital murder in Ohio, to ensure they would never be returned to slavery in Kentucky. Their exact words were that they had rather "go singing to the gallows than be returned to slavery." This jarring proclamation about the gallows has an air of radical defiance that, sadly, is consistent with what Margaret and Mary previously had said about their bondage experience. Because life for the Garners was a kind of "perpetually suspended death sentence," it is no wonder they preferred physical death. Death offered a peace and freedom they could never hope to see in a life in bondage. The Garners sought not only to escape slavery on that January evening but also their painful, humiliating, overworked, bruised, and beaten-down pasts. The outcome of the hearing for them, then, literally was a life-and-death matter.[66]

DEATH SENTENCE

For nearly two weeks, Commissioner Pendery deliberated on the Garners' fate. Then, on February 26, 1856, he rendered his decision, returning all the Garners back to their respective owners. He based his decision on the Supreme Court decision *Strader et al. v. Graham* (1850), which held that if a Kentucky slave owner traveled to Ohio with his slaves, it is "not to be understood as renouncing his right to his slave." Responding to Jolliffe's argument that the Garners were free because the Ohio Constitution prohibited slavery and involuntary servitude, Pendery held that the "true effect of that clause [in the Constitution] being to prevent slavery as an institution within her limits, rather than to execute the act of manumission upon foreign slaves temporarily upon our soil with the master's consent."

Pendery believed that they all had been in Ohio previously, but concluded that Ohio law protects freedom, and does not create or cause it. He said that had the Garners insisted on freedom during their previous visits to Ohio, the state would have protected it, but by returning to Kentucky and slavery with their owners, they "voluntarily abandoned their claims to freedom." With a twinge of empathy for the Garners, Commissioner Pendery concluded his decision, "However painful the result may be to the defendants in this case, it is my duty to deliver them . . . into the custody of the claimant[s]."[67]

The fugitives could not be returned to their owners' custody until the outstanding jurisdictional issues were resolved. Judge Humphrey Leavitt (judge for the US District Court for Southern Ohio) had yet to rule on the custody dispute between the federal and state authorities. Moreover, Probate Judge Burgoyne had issued writs of habeas corpus for the Garner children a week earlier on February 21 that also needed to be heard. On February 28, Judge Leavitt ruled that the federal marshals had the right to custody of the Garners. He explained that Ohio could not issue a habeas corpus for any prisoner already in federal custody; Ohio had no right to interfere. In other words, the US marshals would retain juridical authority over the Garners to finish carrying out the letter of the 1850 Fugitive Slave Act and return them to slavery.[68]

No sooner had Leavitt rendered his decision than the marshals rushed the Garners from their cells, loaded them into an omnibus, and headed to the Covington ferry. James Marshall asked Robert if he was sorry he had run away and asked if he wanted to go back and resume his life in Richwood as it was before, Robert replied that he would not mind going back if he would be treated right and "not knocked about," a clear reference to abuse. A crowd followed the omnibus to the river, but unlike previous crowds, the mood was solemn, with the "silence and order of a funeral procession."[69]

When they arrived on the Covington side of the Ohio River, the Garners were taken to the jail, while their owners, their owners' attorneys, witnesses, marshals, and other supporters celebrated with drinks, revelry, and victory speeches at the Magnolia House hotel in Covington. After speeches from Marshal Robinson and S. T. Moore, one of James Marshall's attorneys, the crowd called for Archibald K. Gaines to give a speech. Not an eloquent man, Gaines allowed another man to speak for him, who explained that he had pursued the Garners out of principle.

As the crowd dispersed, someone recognized Edmond Babb, a reporter for the antislavery-leaning *Cincinnati Daily Gazette,* in their midst. Although proslavery Kentuckians had won the legal battle, apparently that victory was not enough to stem their thirst for abolitionists' blood. Southern gentlemen Archibald K. Gaines and James Marshall spurred the crowd to attack Babb. Someone struck the reporter from behind as he walked toward the river. The crowd quickly surrounded him and people began beating him and shouting, "He's a d—d abolitionist, give him h—ll," and "Take him down to the river, and put him on a cake of ice, and let him go to the d—l." Babb was knocked down, kicked, trampled, and might have been killed or maimed had Ohioans not come to his rescue, drawn their guns, and ordered the mob to stand down.[70] Unfortunately, this would not be the last time Gaines would be implicated in a public beating of a white man in northern Kentucky.

Meanwhile back in Ohio, local officials persisted in trying to bring the Garners back to face murder charges for Mary's murder. On 29 February 1856, Joseph Cox, Hamilton County's prosecuting attorney, sent a letter detailing the case to Ohio's governor, Salmon P. Chase, along with their indictment. The indictment specified that Margaret "purposely and of deliberate and premeditated malice giving to the said Mary Garner . . . a mortal wound of the length of five inches and of the depth of three inches." Chase drafted requisition orders on 4 March and sent them by messengers to Kentucky's governor, Charles S. Morehead. When Governor Morehead received the orders two days later, he issued a warrant for the Garners' arrests.[71] An Ohio extradition and subsequent conviction for murder would have ripped the Garners from their slaveholders' grasps forever. Abolitionists reasoned that bringing the Garners back to face murder charges would ensure they would no longer be enslaved. The irony, of course, is that people believed a murder conviction and possible imprisonment in Ohio to be a better option than slavery in Kentucky. Either way, the Garners were doomed.

Apparently, someone must have tipped Gaines and Marshall off about the arrest warrant, so they hurriedly sent Margaret, Robert, and their children to Louisville, intending to place them on a steamer heading farther south. The warrant was telegraphed to the Louisville sheriff to try to head off the family at the docks, but the slaveholders were two steps ahead. The enslaved Garners already had been placed aboard the *Henry Lewis,* a steamship bound for New Orleans, on the morning of 7 March, just ahead of the warrant.[72] This hasty removal guaranteed that no one would ever be brought to justice for Mary's murder—not Margaret, not Gaines, and not slavery itself.

A day into the journey to New Orleans, the *Henry Lewis* collided with another steamboat, the *Edward Howard,* on the Mississippi River. The impact threw the Garner adults, who had been chained together, into the icy river. With Margaret's hands chained, she could not hold onto Cilla, who had been on her lap before the collision. Cilla drowned, along with two dozen others. According to one report, Margaret expressed "frantic joy" to learn her only surviving daughter now was also dead.[73] Many believed her rejoicing implicated her in Cilla's death. Moreover, it is incomprehensible to some that fate alone would have finished the job that Margaret had intended on 28 January 1856, when she had bashed Cilla in the head with a shovel. The circumstances led to speculations and rumors that she had intentionally drowned the infant, at worst, or failed to save her, at best. The abolitionist newspaper, the *Liberator,* chronicled those rumors in its 21 March 1856 report of the crash. According to one rumor, after the steamers crashed, Margaret had thrown her infant daughter into the river and jumped in after her in an attempted murder-suicide. Another rumor insisted that with Cilla in her arms, Margaret had tried to jump onto a passing boat to escape, but had fallen short, sending them both into the river. We may never know what happened immediately prior to and after the *Henry Lewis* accident, but we do know that Margaret had been handcuffed, and that the impact of the crash had sent her and Cilla into the river. Unable to fight for her own life because she still was in handcuffs, Margaret was saved from drowning by the ship's cook. Both the cook and Robert, who were both present, refuted the idea that Cilla's tragic death had been at Margaret's hands.[74]

Even Cilla's death did not deter Gaines's plans to get the Garners as far from Ohio as quickly as possible. The family was quickly moved to another steamboat and immediately continued its journey down the Mississippi River to his brother's plantation at Gaines Landing, Arkansas— well beyond the reach of Ohio's requisition orders. Rightfully tentative about the rebellious influence the Garner family might have on other enslaved people at Gaines Landing, the Gaines family decided to send them even farther south to yet another brother, Abner LeGrand Gaines, a cotton broker and planter in New Orleans. At some point weeks later, Archibald—bowing to the "infamy" he had earned for his actions—had

Margaret brought back to Covington, Kentucky, on 2 April, presumably to comply with Ohio's requisition orders. She remained in the Kenton County jail between 2 April and 9 April 1856, but Ohio officials were completely unaware she was even there. Archibald K. Gaines did not telegraph Governor Chase to inform him that Margaret was lodged in a Kentucky jail until 8 April; that telegraph stated that he planned to send her away on 10 April if he had not received the governor's requisition orders by then. In response, Chase rushed to draw up new requisition orders. Ohio sheriffs arrived at the Kentucky jail the morning of 10 April intending to pick up the prisoner and deliver her back to Ohio. They learned that Gaines already had, again, spirited Margaret back to New Orleans the previous evening, 9 April. Gaines clearly never intended to hand Margaret over to Ohio officials. He only wanted to appear as if he had made his best effort to cooperate. This flagrant skirting of the law opened Gaines up to criticism and drew disdain from all corners. People began to see him as a dishonorable man. According to one paper: "[Gaines] is regarded with great contempt by all honorable Kentuckians for his conduct in taking Margaret away secretly from Frankfort and selling her down South, when he had promised the Governor of that state [Kentucky] to keep her to await requisition from Governor Chase [Ohio]." By so doing, he had caused Governor Morehead to break his word to Governor Chase, "thus bringing disgrace upon the state."[75] The *Cincinnati Gazette* editorialized, "Why Mr. Gaines brought Margaret back at all, we cannot comprehend. If it was to vindicate his character, he was most unfortunate in the means he selected, for his duplicity has now placed him in worse light than ever before, and kept before the public the miserable spectacle of his dishonor." The abolitionist paper *Liberator*, evaluating what the case had cost Gaines, wrote, "Perhaps he is only a weak man, who felt the impulse to do right, but had not strength to resist temptation to sell—for the price of a negro woman—his honor and his good name, besides bringing disgrace upon his State."[76] In other words, he had traded his honor to keep Margaret.

The primary way that white slaveholding men earned dishonor was through lying, cheating, stealing, and other evidence of poor character and morals. They also lost honor through inappropriate sexual relationships with African American women. It was not the relationships alone or the offspring born of them that brought dishonor, but when those relationships were scandalized, flaunted, or made public. Regardless of whether Gaines's relationship with Margaret was sexual, when he went to great

DRIVEN TOWARD MADNESS

lengths to lie, deceive, and otherwise avoid honoring the requisition orders, he brought himself dishonor. Dishonor's corollary is shame, which is defined as "having honor taken way in a dramatic public display."[77] Mary's death at her mother's hand, the injuries to the other children, the hearing, and the events surrounding the requisitions all constitute dramatic public display. In a society in which white male slaveholders' power and honor were practically unshakeable, it is ironic that women—Margaret Garner, and to a lesser extent Lucy Stone—stripped this slaveholding white male of his honor and baptized him with shame. The former, through her efforts to murder her children, made a powerful implicit negative statement about his character as an owner; the latter, through powerful sexual allegations assailed him as a faithful husband and honorable man.

Often, southern slave owners' public behavior was guided by a desire for honor and a fear of shame.[78] In a desperate bid to regain the honor he had lost, Archibald K. Gaines published a rambling open letter in the 15 April 1856 issue of the proslavery journal, *Cincinnati Daily Enquirer.* He tried to explain why he had sent Margaret away ahead of those requisition orders, but the letter had the opposite effect because it was full of noticeable, threadbare lies, including his erroneous claim that he had announced Margaret's return in Cincinnati papers on 2 April. Even as he lied about critical details of the case, Gaines blamed abolitionists and the local papers for wrongfully damaging his character and honor, Gaines's letter reveals contradictions of thought, action, and character, if not also a shaky grasp on reality:

> I am morally sure that the Abolitionists care nothing for Peggy, either through regard for the offended majesty of the laws of Ohio, or for any sympathy with her as an oppressed, down trodden persecuted, heart-broken, desperate woman; and I am equally sure that the atrocious scoundrels have a wider and meaner object in view—that they care nothing for negroes or their owners, and only wish to use both as material for promotion of political ends, for furtherance of their objects of treason to the Constitution and laws of the Union.[79]

Gaines's hypocritical contradictions are laid bare when he condemns abolitionists for having no sympathy for Margaret "as an oppressed, down trodden persecuted, heart-broken, desperate woman." He goes on to castigate them for "caring nothing for negroes." Clearly, the irony of his letter is that he truly believed that *he* had concern and sympathy for his slaves. This contradiction between keeping people enslaved, on one hand, while claiming to be concerned for their welfare was quite common among slaveholders.

Although Gaines should have felt triumphant about his victory in the court and his subsequent, successful evasion of Ohio's requisition orders, apparently he stewed in anger and resentment for some time afterward. One afternoon in June 1857, Garner attorney John Jolliffe traveled to Covington for a dinner party and happened to run into Archibald K. Gaines on the street while on his way to his friend's home. The men had not seen each other since Commissioner Pendery's ruling one year earlier. They began conversing, but Jolliffe did not immediately recognize the slave owner. When he asked Gaines's name, Gaines thundered, "My name is Gaines. I know you d—d well, you d—d rascal—you d—d nigger thief. You came over here to steal our niggers." Jolliffe sarcastically retorted that he actually had come for dinner. Gaines could not contain his rage and began cursing at Jolliffe and punching him in his chest and face. Jolliffe did not to return any blows, but instead changed his course, and started making his way back to the ferry, intending to return to Cincinnati. Gaines followed on his heels, bellowing that the attorney "was a d—d nigger thief, and that all those interested in niggers had better look out, for he had come over to steal their niggers." His shouting attracted thugs and others eager to see or join a fight. The disorderly crowd followed the rivals toward the river. Jolliffe appealed to the onlookers' gentlemanly instincts to protect him, but instead they mocked him and barked menacing recommendations of "lynch him," "cowhide him," and "hang him." Encouraged by these calls for violence, Gaines asked for a cowhide whip. Cowhide whips, or long strips of dried ox hide, were designed to cut the flesh, draw blood, and scar victims and were commonly used against animals and slaves. Using one on a white man was incredibly debasing and humiliating. Someone in the crowd passed Gaines one of these whips and he raised it, and whipped it, striking Jolliffe on his back. Fortunately, a deputy marshal who witnessed the assault quickly arrested Gaines on the spot.[80]

Gaines's attack on the abolitionist attorney can be distinguished from other antiabolitionist violence in the region. Antiabolitionists, or proslavery supporters who despised abolitionists and abolitionism, used mob violence to scare, punish, disrupt, and impede their antislavery activism.

An unholy alliance of "gentlemen" of property and standing and unskilled laborers who owned neither property nor slaves, antiabolitionists on both sides of the river had a history of committing mob violence against abolitionists, for example, when they hunted down the abolitionist editor James G. Birney in the streets of Cincinnati in 1836, intending to tar and feather him. Unable to find him, the mob settled on breaking into the office of his journal, the *Philanthropist,* where they broke the presses and threw the pieces into the Ohio River. A year later in Alton, Illinois, an antiabolitionist mob murdered the abolitionist journalist Elijah Lovejoy.[81] Jolliffe's attack was different; it was not committed at the hands of a bloodthirsty mob, but by Gaines alone. It was personal.

Obviously feeling humiliated and dishonored by the lingering effects of the sexual insinuations, damning attacks on his character during the Garner hearing, and his own duplicity, Gaines had gone after Jolliffe, in part, to avenge his honor. Jolliffe had rather persuasively castigated Gaines and Marshall as slave owners during the hearing, accusing one of having little Mary's blood on his hands and of cannibalism. After the hearing, what had been left of Gaines's honor eroded when he broke his promise to have the Garners available for Ohio's requisition and, instead, hurriedly and surreptitiously shipped them down the river—twice! In the antebellum South, a person's word was his honor, and Gaines had broken his and operated deceitfully. Seeing the Garners' attorney nearly a year later may have reminded Gaines of his embarrassment and lost honor and pushed him to that "inarticulate fury."[82] His impulsive violence against his social equals surely can leave no doubts that he did this and worse to Margaret Garner during the six years he held her in bondage in Kentucky.

"FADED FACES" TELL SECRETS—OR DO THEY?

I am black, you see,—
And the babe who lay on my bosom so,
Was far too white . . . too white for me;
As white as the ladies who scorned to pray
Beside me at church but yesterday;
Though my tears had washed a place for my knee.

My own, own child! I could not bear
To look in his face, it was so white.
I covered him up with a kerchief there;
I covered his face in close and tight:
And he moaned and struggled, as well might be,
For the white child wanted his liberty—
Ha, ha! he wanted his master right.

—Elizabeth Barrett Browning, 1848[1]

Beyond the Garners' untold physical and psycho-logical abuse, an additional layer of abuse was submerged: sexual. Presumed sexual abuse has been a prominent undercurrent in the histories about Margaret Garner. Allegations about Gaines's sexual exploitation of Margaret were first raised by Lucy Stone during the fugitive slave hearing. In open court, she had given a speech that laid bare the most controversial core of the entire tragedy—rape and race mixing—when she declared, "The faded faces of the negro children tell too plainly to what degradation female slaves submit. Rather than give her little daughter to that life, she killed it."[2] Stone bluntly stated—as none but a women's rights advocate would dare—that the Garner children's light complexions, or "faded faces," testified to Margaret's "degradation"— which in the nineteenth century, was a euphemism for sexual abuse. In one declaration, Stone not only had accused Gaines of sexual abuse and insinuated his paternity of Margaret's children, but also explained that the hell Margaret tried to save her daughters from was sexual abuse. Writing later, Stone's daughter and biographer, Alice Stone Blackwell, recounted what her mother had shared with her in support of this claim: "Margaret had tried to kill all her children, but she had made sure of the little girl." She did not want her to "suffer as she had."[3] In short, Stone insisted that Mary's murder had been a gendered mercy killing, of sorts.

Had Margaret Garner really told Stone that she had been raped by Gaines and that he fathered her daughters, as Stone implied?[4] Perhaps; perhaps not. Garner may have felt comfortable enough with Stone to confess these salacious secrets. After all, Stone had an empathetic ear: not only was she a women's rights advocate and abolitionist, but she fully empathized with Garner's decision to kill her daughter. But Stone's accusations complicate this history and lead to at least two plausible theories of what happened to Garner.

The question of whether Margaret Garner had a sexual relationship with Archibald K. Gaines, and if it constituted rape, cannot be known with absolute certainty. The answer cannot be disentangled from nineteenth-century gender and racial assumptions; nor can it be disentangled from how social and economic power—and powerlessness—functioned in nineteenth-century society. At one end of the power spectrum were powerful white men, who wielded unchecked racial, gender, and economic power in southern society—power that was protected and magnified by the legal system. The intersection of power, ownership, and patriarchy left enslaved women vulnerable to all manner of abuse and brutality.

At the other end of the spectrum, enslaved people were powerless and considered chattel—property that could be bought and sold in the marketplace. African American women, in particular, were treated as "purchasable sexual and economic commodities."[5] When a man purchased a bondswoman, he also purchased the right to have sex with her. The business transaction that completed her sale is all that it took to open the door to unlimited and unchecked sexual access to her. In antebellum slave society, ownership, power, and sexual access were inextricably linked as it related to owners. Gaines owned Garner's *body:* it was his to do with what he wanted, regardless of her will or desires. And no one could stop him—not even the law.

In the nineteenth century, the legal (but heteronormative and raced) definition of rape was "carnal knowledge of a woman forcibly and against her will." In order to convict an alleged rapist, officials needed to prove that the sexual intercourse occurred by force, or with some violence, and against the woman's will.[6] Everything about slavery was maintained by violence and done against enslaved people's wills; sex was no exception. Slaveholders owned the bodies, and ordered the movements of their bondspeople. The intertwined elements of ownership, abuse, and power, meant that sex with those with stark powerlessness—like enslaved women—sometimes made physical force unnecessary. Owners used coercive tactics to obtain sex and sexual favors from them in a myriad of ways, including threats of violence. In fact, the threat of violence was second to violence as a form of sexual coercion. Violence was so pervasive in slave culture, that the threat of violence often is all it took to get these women to submit to sex. Slave owners controlled the provisions, punishments, workload, quality of life, and stability of slaves' families, so they could deny or threaten any aspect of their lives to get a woman to submit sexually. Sometimes, too, promises of rewards and leniency were used for the same ends. For example, an owner could demand sex in exchange for visitation rights to loved ones, for better food, or time off.[7] In short, enslaved women had no real choices about whether they would or would not engage in sex with their owners. Because of this lack of real choices, all sex between an unfree woman and her owner can be considered nonconsensual.[8]

Kentucky, though, did not make force, violence, or the woman's consent the standard to define rape; race was the first standard. Kentucky law defined rape as to "unlawfully and carnally know any *white* [emphasis added] woman, against her will or consent."[9] In other words, only white women could be victims of rape in the eyes of the law; only men who raped *them* were rapists. This standard meant that even if Garner had gone to officials complaining of sexual abuse, the existing structure of the law did not allow her rapist to be arrested or convicted. Certainly, one cannot ignore the legal and social realities of the world in which she lived.

DRIVEN TOWARD MADNESS

As an enslaved person, an African American, and a woman, Margaret Garner belonged to three groups of disempowered people. The intersection of patriarchy, white supremacy, and wealth meant that as a white male slave owner, Gaines had all the power. The intersection of race, gender, and enslaved status meant that Margaret's powerlessness had a multiplicative effect on her oppression. Consequently, she was vulnerable to sexual assault at the hands of her owner and any other white man, for that matter. The very laws of the land did not protect enslaved African American women in that powerlessness, making them even more vulnerable. For example, in nineteenth-century America, there were statutes against raping white women—some even raised the death penalty for such an offense, but none specifically prohibited the rape of African American women. When enslaved women were raped by anyone besides their owners, the owners could press charges against the perpetrator, but not for *rape*. Such rapists would—at best, only be charged with *trespassing* because enslaved women were legally regarded as property.[10] There were a handful of southern communities where men accused of raping black women and girls were arrested under the existing statutes against white women. Even though white men in such places could be arrested for raping enslaved women, convictions were rare. In order to convict a man for raping an enslaved woman, several legal barriers had to be met. First, a white person with some social or economic power had to bring the charges before officials. Then, a magistrate had to believe the complaint was credible and prosecutable. Finally, a jury would need to determine the guilt of the accused. Those barriers in a racist society blocked justice for these women. Between 1700 and the time of this case in 1856, not one white man had been convicted of raping an enslaved woman, reinforcing the fact that African American women and girls were afforded no legal protection or justice. Slaveholders and other elite men easily avoided both prosecution and conviction. What this also tells us is that a slave owner's social and economic power to sexually abuse enslaved women with impunity made sexual abuse a privilege granted through slavery, ownership, socioeconomic status, and even whiteness.[11]

To add insult to injury, enslaved women could not even expect redress if they were assaulted by an *enslaved* male. Masters rarely pursued legal punishment in such cases and usually just handled the matters themselves. Hence, African American women were simultaneously the most sexually vulnerable and legally unprotected class in antebellum society, bar none.

The absence of statutes in most locales, coupled with the failure to convict men of sexually abusing them in others, is the equivalent of rendering them "unrapable" in the eyes of the law.[12] In the final analysis, Margaret was vulnerable to sexual abuse because she was an unprotected, powerless, and legally "unrapable" enslaved woman.

Detrimental stereotypes and mischaracterizations about African American women influenced people's willingness to believe rape claims and dulled sympathy for them as victims. The prevailing antebellum assumptions about them cast them as hypersexed and "open" by nature, and willing to have sexual intercourse at a moment's notice, without reservation or discrimination. These assumptions not only made black women vulnerable to rape, but precluded sympathy for them as victims. Their presumed promiscuity and hypersexuality made many whites believe that they initiated sexual contact—as temptresses, or jezebels. These pernicious ideas were used to explain to those outside the South the high numbers of enslaved biracial children in southern slave quarters.[13] Ironically, the jezebel stereotype implies that black women were not fully powerless: it depicted them as having "power" not only to draw powerful patriarchs into bed, but to choose the father of their children. Of course, this is the furthest thing from the truth, but the myth explains why people then and now have had trouble digesting the possibility that Margaret Garner's children were the product of rape. In sum, Archibald K. Gaines had the freedom to do with "his negro woman" (as Gaines and Richwood residents referred to Margaret) what he wanted.[14]

As history has demonstrated, opportunity abounded for sexual assaults. Enslaved women who did women's work in the home, including cooking, cleaning, and caring for a man's family, were easy prey. There was little deterrent inside the male slaveholder's household—even white women—to prevent him from taking advantage of enslaved women. The Gaines women, specifically, were relatively powerless to stop any potential abuse, sexual or otherwise, even if they had been inclined to intervene. In 1856, Archibald's mother, Elizabeth, was eighty-two years old. The only other adult Gaines woman at Maplewood was his wife, Elizabeth.[15] If the Gaines women were aware of any sexual abuse, they likely would have been disinclined to confront the patriarch—especially given his history of impulsivity and violence. It is also possible that the Gaines women physically abused Margaret, although probably not sexually. Historians have exposed that slave-owning women committed all manners of violence against enslaved people. Some of these women delivered particularly vicious and cruel beatings that left permanent scars or injuries. The findings in this case do not implicate the Gaines women in the violence against Margaret or any other Maplewood slaves; but even if they did not mete out beatings themselves, slave-owning women may have engaged in threats of damnation for disobedience, verbal insults, pinching, slapping, hair pulling, burnings, scratching, denying food or sleep, kicking, and so on.[16] In sum, the Gaines women may not be blameless in Margaret Garner's enslavement experience, despite the historical silences.

The truth is, if Margaret Garner were being sexually abused, she had no protectors at Maplewood, in Richwood, or in Boone County. Only her own physical resistance could have stopped attempts to sexually abuse her on any given day; nothing but her full escape from slavery, or death, could permanently have ended the threat of sexual abuse at the hands of her owner. Those were her options.

Psychologists and criminal profilers today agree that there are multiple types of men who rape women for a variety of reasons, including sexual fantasies, anger, rejection, or sadistic impulses. Anger retaliatory rapists harbor hardened negative views of women. They are impulsive with explosive tempers. These rapists aim to hurt or degrade the victim. Anger retaliatory rapists tend to attack spontaneously and often brutalize their victims. Power reassurance rapists tend to be loners who are woefully deficient in social skills and confidence. They are nonathletic and passive. The power reassurance rapist believes the victim is a willing participant in the sexual act. By contrast, power assertive rapists have extreme beliefs of superiority over the victim (often gendered, but could also be racial). The power assertive rapist tends to be hypermacho, hypermasculine, athletic, and confident and participates in a subculture that degrades women, such as sports or fraternities. The goal of this type of rapist is to dominate women or put them in their place. The most important characteristic that these typologies share is that they are inclined to violence and have committed violence in other areas of their lives. Rape itself is an act of violence, with sex as the vehicle for that agression.[17]

Was Archibald K. Gaines capable of rape? Certainly, he possessed qualities in each of these typologies of rapists. For example, he was embarrassingly deficient in social skills, especially speaking skills, and repeatedly shrank from opportunities to speak publicly. Although James Marshall had spoken at Gaines's hearing, he had not done the same for his friend—likely due to an aversion to public speaking. On a couple of occasions, including after the ruling in his case, Gaines had used a proxy to speak for him at his celebration toast. In addition, Gaines was an impulsive man with an explosive and violent temper.

In nineteenth-century trials of alleged rapists, the defendant's character was significant—especially when other evidence was thin. Juries then used an accused man's lifelong character as evidence that could point to his guilt or innocence.[18] We should hold Gaines by the same standard of his day; his history proves he was a violent, controlling, exacting, and vengeful man who had little respect for his equals, much less his social inferiors. Margaret Garner's scarred face is highly suggestive of his violent temper. In addition to sexual assault being a form of violence, it can also accompany physical or emotional abuse. At times, too, physical abuse could be meted out to a woman who resists sexual advances. In fact, history is littered with other examples of enslaved women who endured untold abuse for resisting sexual violence. In a separate incident, when Martha Allen's mother refused to have sex with her owner in North Carolina, he hit her in the head with a piece of wood. Similarly, when young Louisa Picquet avoided her stalker's advances, he whipped her naked with a cowhide strap. The details of her beating border on sexual sadism. She only escaped a worse fate at her owner's hands when the sheriff seized his property for bad debts.[19] Were the scars on Margaret Garner's face sustained when she refused to submit to Gaines sexually? We may never know, but those scars leave no doubt about the physical terrorism—if not also sexual terrorism—under which Margaret Garner lived.

Margaret is not the only one who may have suffered violence at Gaines's hands. His first wife, Margaret Ann Dudley, allegedly had died from injuries sustained during a fall, but people had long speculated whether she actually sustained them at Gaines's hands during a beating.[20] Second, Gaines had provoked a Kentucky mob to brutally beat a Cincinnati reporter with antislavery leanings. In addition, a year after he emerged victorious from the fugitive slave hearing, Gaines verbally and physically assaulted attorney John Jolliffe with a cowhide whip in the streets of Covington, Kentucky. If Gaines did not hesitate about beating a white man in broad daylight, one can assume that he did much worse to his own bondspeople who were his social, economic, and political inferiors.[21] Hence, potential sexual abuse, as an act of violence, is entirely consistent with Gaines's violent past. These multiple incidents of violence speak volumes about Gaines's aggression, hostility, violence, and impulsivity.

Closely related to the questions about sexual abuse, the other huge question at the center of the case is whether Archibald K. Gaines was the biological father of some of Margaret Garner's children. There is no way to absolutely prove the paternity of her children now—more than one hundred and fifty years after her death, especially now that the Garner lineage has historically disappeared. There are, however, clues that he fathered one or more of Margaret Garner's children. Although there are no absolute smoking guns, legal historian Annette Gordon-Reed reminds historians that proof and evidence are two different concepts; she insists that each individual item of evidence "does not itself add up to proof," but "goes toward *establishing* proof."[22] Little pieces of evidence taken together build a mountain of evidence that proves Gaines fathered one or more of Margaret's children.

In the nineteenth century, long before DNA-based paternity testing, the next best way to prove or disprove paternity was to determine whether the alleged father had access to the mother at the time of conception.[23] Because we do not know the exact dates of birth for Margaret's children, we cannot definitively say that Gaines was with her in a given month of conception.[24] But as her owner, his unlimited and unrestrained access to her makes paternity of her children highly possible. In fact, Gaines had greater access to Margaret than her own husband, Robert, who lived on another farm and did not see her every day, and was frequently hired out far from Richwood.

Another piece of evidence that goes toward proving Gaines's paternity is the skin shade of Margaret's daughters. Local newspapers described Margaret as "mulatto, showing from one- fourth to one-third white blood," which means she had a light complexion—lighter than average African Americans. Sam, her younger son, is also described as a "mulatto" in some reports, "negro" in others. Robert and their eldest son, Tommy, were described as "negro," which in nineteenth-century terms meant they had medium brown to dark brown complexions. Cilla is described as "much lighter in color than herself [Margaret]—light enough to show a red tinge in its cheeks." Margaret's deceased daughter, Mary, is described as "almost white—and was a little girl of rare beauty."[25] Reporters wrote painstakingly detailed descriptions of the complexions and physical features of Margaret and her children because they mattered—to the reporters and to the reading public. For sure, these descriptions of color, facial features, and percentage of white blood are full of social meaning and implications.

In the antebellum era, Kentucky legally classified a person as African American if he or she had an "appreciable admixture" of African American blood. In other words, if there were visible traces of African American ancestry, then that person would be legally defined as African American. When not applying that standard, Kentucky held to a one-sixteenth rule, meaning if the person in question had even one great-great-grandparent who was African American, he or she would legally be classified as African American.[26] The one-sixteenth rule, which is similar to the one-drop rule, effectively meant that if a person had an African American ancestor, that person was legally defined as African American. This legal definition teaches us that in antebellum Kentucky, fractions, drops, and "appreciable admixtures" mattered. Typically, they mattered in proving blackness, but curiously, in the Margaret Garner case the fractions and drops hinted at degrees of whiteness (observers noted fractions of whiteness she had: "showing from one-fourth to one-third white blood").

Whites generally determined racial identity in several ways in this era: documented ancestry, ascriptive identity (in other words, the performance of racial identity and what people assume one's racial identity is: you were black if you associated with blacks), scientific definitions (how medical and science experts classified and distinguished the races), slave status (most assumed that all enslaved people were African American and that all African Americans were enslaved or had been enslaved), and physical appearance.[27] In trials that centered on racial identity, witnesses carefully described people's skin color and other features as a way of assigning them to a racial category or indicating their ancestry. Affixing fractions and degrees of whiteness to Margaret and her children and using words and phrases such as "almost white" with a "red tinge" in one child's cheeks were coded and polite ways for the reporter to imply that the girls had white ancestry in their family tree. Skin color descriptors and percentages of whiteness did more than imply white ancestry; they also identified the generation when white blood entered into the equation. The implication is that Margaret Garner, who was estimated to have between one-fourth and one-third white blood, had at least a white grandparent, while it is implied that her "almost white" daughter, Mary, had a white father.[28] And that is how white Kentuckians then talked about race-mixing and white ancestry without explicitly leveling any accusations.[29]

Visual descriptions of skin color are important, but cannot be used as the only and absolute proof of paternity because such observations were not scientific then. Although scientists now use reflectance spectrophotometers to measure the lightness of skin shade, in 1856 people simply made visual observations, which were purely subjective, inconsistent, based on slippery and inconsistent definitions of mulatto, and often steeped in racism, if not also colorism.[30] Additionally, the use of the term mulatto is loaded. It could be used to refer to skin shade, biraciality, or, more often, both. Moreover, the term is also imprecise and subjective: this is one reason why one census taker or other observer could classify a person of African descent as "negro" and another would classify the same person as "mulatto," as with the conflicting descriptors of Sammy Garner. With the vast diversity of skin shades among people of African descent, our color lexicon and accompanying vocabulary is inadequate not only to name each of those hues, but to distinguish them from one another. Consequently, skin shade observations cannot be taken at face value by themselves, especially because racism then colored so much of how people read black and brown bodies. Hence, we cannot know with any scientific certainty how light the Garner children actually were; even if we could, we may not all agree because of subjectivity. Because each person read African Americans' complexions differently and states defined what it meant to be mulatto differently, there is no way to categorize them with any precision now.[31]

Although melanin inherited through genes is the main contributor to shade of skin, *non*-genetic factors, including sensitivity to sun exposure, environmental factors, and vitamin deficiencies, are other factors that determine the darkness or lightness of one's complexion. Besides that, skin complexion is not stable over time: African American infants are born lighter and get darker with sun exposure, for example.[32] So it is possible that the Garner daughters, being so young, simply still had not gotten their full color yet, which explains some fairness of complexion, but not all. In short, we must take historical white observations about the Garners' skin color with a grain of imprecise and unscientific salt. Color observations coupled with genetics are stronger evidence of paternity in this case, though.

Outside of geneticists, most people have little to no understanding of how genes actually determine skin pigmentation. Science has evolved by leaps and bounds in the areas of genetics and heredity since 1856, and that new knowledge should inform this case. We no longer need to rely on old wives' tales or hypothesize that rare events in nature are more common than they are. We now know that skin pigmentation is an inherited trait and that multiple genes—or polygenic inheritance—collectively determine the skin pigmentation hue individuals inherit. Anywhere from three to six different additive genes determine a person's level of skin pigmentation. Dominant skin color genes produce high amounts of a polymer called melanin, which is what gives skin its dark color. These genes are additive, meaning the more dark skin color genes one inherits, the darker the complexion. According to geneticists, a person who inherits all dominant darker skin color genes from their parents will have the darkest skin shading. Most people inherit some recessive alleles of these genes; recessive alleles do not yield as much melanin and will produce lighter skin. People who inherit all recessive alleles from their parents will have the lightest of skin colors: white or near-white skin. Those are the two poles, though. Biracial people—or mulattoes as they were called then—have a genotype which has equal number of dominant and recessive alleles and will have an intermediate skin shading.[33]

All of this means, then, that skin pigmentation can be predicted mathematically.[34] Margaret Garner was described as a "mulatto, showing from one-fourth to one-third white blood" and "chestnut colored."[35] Based on these descriptions, one can conclude she was a shade of light—or "chestnut"—brown. Her husband was described by observers as "negro" and as having a "black complexion." When whites in the antebellum era used the term "negro" when referring to skin complexion, it simply meant that the person had medium to dark brown skin and no visible evidence of white ancestry. It is possible that two African Americans can produce a child who receives all, or most, of the light skin color genes from both parents and be significantly lighter than either parent, or receive all or most of the darker skin color genes from both parents and be significantly darker than either parent.[36] This could explain how Margaret and Robert Garner had daughters who were much fairer in complexion than they.

Although we cannot predict how many dark or light skin shade genes an infant will get, when light and dark skin color individuals mate, their offspring typically are a blend of the two. In layman's terms, if an infant has two biracial parents of light brown skin tones, there is a 50 percent probability that its skin pigmentation will be a blend of its parents' colors; while there is a 25 percent chance that its skin pigment would be darker and a 25 percent chance that it would be lighter than both parents'.[37] In other words, Margaret and Robert would only have a 25 percent chance of having a child lighter than they. But just how light that child could get is a different question.

If one examines the specific details of this case, the gnawing question that emerges is what are the chances that these two African Americans could produce a child who is as near-white in skin tone as Mary and Cilla were described? According to those who specialize in skin tone science, such an occurrence is exceedingly rare—even today. Only 1 out of 500, or 0.2 percent, of children born to African American parents would produce a child who looks white. People described Margaret's and Robert's skin tones as light brown and medium brown, respectively. When light brown and medium brown skin genotypes are plugged into a three-gene Punnett Square (which predicts the genetic possibilities of offspring), 64 possible genotype combinations for their offspring emerge. The probability that Robert and Margaret could produce a child who was phenotypically (or visibly) nearly white, is between zero and 6.3 percent, at best.[38] In other words, it is genetically possible, although highly unlikely and rare, that Margaret and Robert as they were described would have produced a child who appeared to be "almost white" as people described Mary.[39] It is more probable and likely, though, that a white man fathered the girls. Geneticists assert that "as long as one parent is white and is [consequently] contributing light skin color genes, the child will always be lighter in color than the mulatto parent."[40] Such a pairing would yield a child who was very fair in complexion (lighter than its mother), as Mary was described. In other words, the combination of a white father and a so-called mulatto mother is more likely to yield children with Mary and Cilla's complexions than is a pairing like Margaret and Robert.[41]

The lighter complexions of Mary and Cilla would indicate a white man as the putative father; but that does not necessarily mean that that white man was Archibald K. Gaines. As an enslaved woman, her body could be used by any white man who desired her for sexual purposes. Owners, their sons, other male relatives, and employees posed the greatest sexual threat to enslaved women. Several white men had access to Margaret Garner. Archibald's younger brother, as well as one of his wife's brothers, also lived at Maplewood at times. During the fugitive slave hearing in Cincinnati, no fewer than half a dozen white men testified that they knew her, including several relatives, neighbors, a physician, and men who worked for Gaines. Peter Nolan, for example, testified that he had worked at Gaines's farm for five years and even had lived there for a year. Clearly, his easy access to Margaret Garner cannot be ignored. Moreover, another white man, John Ashbrook, who routinely purchased livestock from Gaines, also testified that he had frequented the farm and knew Margaret quite well.[42] Although other white men had access to Margaret Garner and possibly could have fathered her children, no man on earth had more sexual access than Archibald K. Gaines, not even her own husband.

If we continue to build this wall of evidence proving Gaines as the father of one or some of Margaret's children, his behavior related to the children cannot be ignored. Gaines's last command to deputies before they broke into the Kite home to reclaim his slaves that January morning was that no laws be broken and "no harm whatever should be done to the little children."[43] In no uncertain terms, he made it clear that their safety was tantamount to that of the adults. Why did he place a premium on their safety? After all, children were less valuable on the open slave market and were yet too young to work and be productive. In other words, they had less financial and productive value to him than the adults. It is clear that they held an emotional value to him, though. In fact, it transcends the typical feelings even so-called benevolent owners had for their bonds-people. Added to that is another instance of Gaines's unusual concern for the Garner children, as outlined in Steven Weisenburger's book. After the slaying, while the other Garners were being loaded up to be taken to court, Gaines was busy loading Mary's body up to take back to Kentucky for a burial. He was preoccupied with that, hardly noticing that the Garners' omnibus had left the scene—an oddity, given how desperate he had been to recover them just hours before. This is all highly suggestive that he cared for the child as a father would.[44]

One cannot discuss this case without acknowledging that there was neither an admission nor a witness to any sexual abuse of Margaret Garner by Archibald K. Gaines. The most glaring silence, of course, is from Margaret Garner herself, who never publicly admitted to, or implied, any sexual abuse or that Gaines was the father of some of her children. Interestingly, too, none of the other Garners ever even insinuated that Gaines had raped her. Robert Garner would have been aware of his wife's torment, and yet years after Margaret and other players including slavery itself were dead, he never as much as even hinted that his wife had been raped by Gaines or that the slave owner may have fathered some of the children. Nor did Gaines ever acknowledge, admit, or deny the allegations. Furthermore, it is also curious that not even one white Richwood resident ever testified to or insinuated the possibility that Gaines had had any sexual contact with Margaret—much less fathered her children.[45] All of those silences taken together threaten to be exculpatory for Gaines.

However, on deeper analysis and contextualization, it is clear these silences do not necessarily mean that Gaines is innocent of the allegations. Each silence must be analyzed in its historical context with sensitivity and perspective. There are multiple possible reasons for Garner's reticence. First, it should come as no surprise that Margaret would remain reticent about rape because most rapes then and now go unreported. Sexual abuse survivors remain silent because they fear reprisals, shame, or scorn, or because they have little faith in the justice system—especially if the perpetrator is an elite man. Moreover, rape survivors of all ethnic and socioeconomic backgrounds sometimes self-impose silence to protect themselves from revisiting the trauma. Historian Darlene Clark Hine reminds us that among black women rape and the threat of rape lead to a "culture of dissemblance," whereby on the surface, survivors have the appearance of openness and full disclosure, but on the inside they "shield the truth of their inner lives and selves from their oppressors." For other survivors, the silence is chosen to avoid a negative social response to their claims. Specifically, it is meant to shield the survivor from societal harm and additional figurative rapes from those who tend to blame the victim, question her veracity, or bring her character or past into question. Besides that, some enslaved women failed to discuss the paternity of their children for a multiplicity of reasons. Margaret's silences could be explained by all of those possibilities.[46]

Beyond possible inner reasons, Margaret Garner's silence may simply have been driven by the social context in which she lived. She lived in a world that did not condemn, charge, or convict white men for raping black women. Such an idea was beyond comprehension for women like her. Hence, she may not have even imagined speaking truth to power. Taken even further, Garner may not have believed that she *could* do anything to stop Gaines from abusing her besides fleeing; because truthfully, she could not.

After Lucy Stone's inflammatory public accusation, neither Gaines nor his attorney, Colonel Francis T. Chambers, raised any objections, or in any way addressed it. Although Stone had—in poor taste, according to southern decorum—ripped away the veil of secrecy that governed amalgamation (contemporary phrase for race-mixing), and with it Gaines's right to put on the mantle of honor, decency, and piety, his legal team failed to acknowledge or address the jarring allegations of rape and race-mixing she raised. Such accusations threatened the reputations and honor of better men, yet Gaines and his attorney remained silent in the face of such charges of sexual impropriety.

Gaines's silence in the face of Stone's incendiary allegations is consistent with how southern men typically responded to accusations that they had sexual relations with enslaved women. Insinuations of infidelity, rape, and race-mixing threatened to dishonor him. Under such a cloud, the only way for him to preserve his honor was not to acknowledge or address the accusations about illicit liaisons with an enslaved woman. It was the only thing a so-called honorable man could do. Founding father Thomas Jefferson, for example, also never acknowledged or addressed the insinuations and allegations of race-mixing against him, and those were later proven true with DNA.[47]

One might have expected Elizabeth Gaines, his wife, to refute the allegations about her husband. However, such allegations and suspicions rendered nineteenth-century Southern white women of the slaveholding class impotent and silent—partly for cultural, gendered, and financial reasons. Women rarely left their husbands in the nineteenth century; one reason is that Victorian gender conventions stigmatized divorcées. Their own personal betrayal often was not enough to get them to be confrontational or even leave their husbands in the face of such revelations. They would have been reluctant to break up their family or raise their children as single mothers. Such things were rare, then. Sometimes, too, these women chose not to confront an abusive man out of fear of his wrath. Finally, Southern white women—especially slaveholding women—were quite dependent on their husbands financially. In that era, there were few options for such women to provide for themselves if they ended their marriages, so many stayed and bore the disgrace of being married to a man whom they knew had had sexual relations with his bondswomen. Unable to act, many of these women turned a blind eye and pretended to be unaware of what was happening, because the cost of confronting misbehaving husbands was simply too high.[48]

Gaines's attorney did indirectly address the allegations of his paternity of Margaret's children when he questioned Dr. Elijah Smith Clarkson, the

Gaines family physician. Dr. Clarkson testified that he knew the entire Gaines family and was familiar with some of his bondspeople, including Peggy—whom he had known since she was two—her oldest two children, and her mother, Cilla. Gaines's attorney asked the doctor if Simon Jr.— Robert—was the father of Peggy's children, Clarkson coolly responded, "We admit that."[49] Because the substance of his testimony had no direct information about Margaret's escape, the capital murder she had committed while in Ohio, or the allegations that she had been to Ohio previously, it is obvious that the sole purpose of calling him to testify was to indirectly address the elephant in the room: the looming question of the paternity of Margaret's children. As a physician, Dr. Clarkson's testimony would appear to be authoritative; in other words, if a doctor testifies that Robert Garner was the father of the children, people would be convinced it was true. Hence, Dr. Clarkson's testimony allowed Gaines to assert Robert's paternity of the children.

Silences among other Boone County residents are also instructive. Certainly, members of that local community would have known better than outsiders what sexual sins had been committed at Maplewood. Richwood was such a small place that such scandalous gossip about interracial sex would have been impossible to contain on Maplewood or even in the larger county—especially after the scrutiny by the press during the hearing. And yet the residents of that small community were conspicuously silent and evaded the topic altogether when discussing the case publicly. The silences in the local historical record are so deafening that it is tantamount to a compact of collective and conspicuous silence.

There was an imperative for a compact of collective and conspicuous silence among white Richwood citizens, though. First, southerners in small towns did not necessarily approve of interracial sex between slave owners and enslaved women, but they were willing to turn a blind eye as long as it was done with discretion and was not part of a bigger pattern of other unethical or dishonorable behavior. It was not the interracial intercourse itself, but the flaunting of such illicit unions, that white southerners deemed objectionable. What southern whites would not tolerate was a slave owner who tried to force them to accept his African American paramour as his wife or endow his mulatto children with the rights and status of white people. For example, Washington society bristled when another Kentuckian, Congressman Richard Mentor Johnson, brought his mulatto daughters with him to social events in the nation's capital, because that was considered to be flaunting his illicit behavior.[50] Gaines—a devout, married man who strived for honor—would have thought better of either flaunting his sexual relationship with Margaret or forcing others to accept her fair-complexioned children as anything more than his property. Hence, the same unwritten southern code that forbade slave owners from flaunting their interracial sexual relationships may have silenced all parties during the hearing.

Another reason Richwood residents would have been reluctant to publicly confirm the allegations made against Gaines at the hearing is that they respected his family or even believed he had some honor—which goes far in explaining why his neighbors and close friends testified and wrote editorials in his defense. But simply because his neighbors believed him to be an honorable man does not mean that he was in fact honorable. Gaines could be an honorable man by the standards of nineteenth-century Boone County, Kentucky, and also be dishonorable in the eyes of others. People outside of that community did not see him with the same eyes as his neighbors. The editors of the abolitionist journal *Liberator* as well as the *Cincinnati Daily Commercial,* for example, believed him to be a liar and wholly dishonorable when he lied about having made Margaret available for extradition to Ohio.[51] These disparities of perception prove the standards for honor were local and situational.

An additional consideration is that speaking publicly about the violence and moral bankruptcy that underpinned the institution of slavery, slave owners, and slave society was considered a huge violation of community and community honor. In many small, white, southern slave communities like Richwood, Kentucky, residents rallied to support one another against outside attacks on their community, its members, or their way of life. The Margaret Garner tragedy brought the entire weight of abolitionist and national scrutiny onto that community. Residents may not have approved of what Gaines had done, but he was one of their own—right or wrong, he belonged to them. So the community closed ranks and built a fortress of support around him—support that included defending him in the media and refusing to bring shame or dishonor to him by publicly acknowledging his paternity of some of Margaret Garner's children or his cruelty to her.[52]

A final factor that may explain the silences in the white Richwood historical record is the culture of silence that governed nineteenth-century discussions of race mixing and sexual assault—singularly or linked. In nineteenth-century white society—in the North and the South—such discussions were taboo. Nineteenth-century notions of modesty and respectability made most people shun public discussions about sex altogether, but especially about nonconsensual or interracial sex. The silence in Richwood was magnified on a regional level. Southern papers' decision not to carry the story at all or minimize its significance underscores how uneasy most felt about talking about these issues.[53] A more interesting observation about the compact of collective and conspicuous silence from white Richwood residents is that not one person ever defended Gaines against the sexual allegations and insinuations. Of the many letters written by his neighbors and friends in his defense and published in Covington newspapers, most of them refute only the accusations that he was a cruel master. At least a few go beyond that and impugn the characters of Margaret and Robert Garner. But none of these defenders refute the allegations of sexual abuse, implicitly or explicitly.[54] And *that* silence speaks volumes.

The "transcendent silence" surrounding this case may not have been intended to protect Gaines or even to conceal his wrongdoings, but to protect honor itself.[55] This horrific case touches on so many taboos and dishonorable elements for southern whites that it was literally unutterable—even for those merely speaking about or reporting on the case. Silence, then, may have been a means to circumvent the embarrassment and humiliation that the case brought to Gaines, his friends and family, Richwood, Boone County, and ultimately, Kentucky.

In the final analysis, the Garner children's "faded faces" mattered to this case, because skin color mattered in antebellum society. People took pains to describe the drops, fractions, and "appreciable admixtures" of whiteness—or blackness—and the nuanced differences between African Americans' skin tones because they mattered. Skin shade colored the discourse and coded how people spoke about interracial sex and even paternity. The volatile intersection of enslavement, gender, and light skin color proved very dangerous to the Garner women in one way or the other.

5 DRIVEN BY MADNESS, BADNESS, OR SADNESS?

Well I know no stronger yearning than a mother's love can be—
I could do and dare forever for the babe upon my knee!
And I feel no deeper sorrow could the light of life eclipse,
Than to see death's shadow settle in its brow and faded lips.
Yet (oh, God of Heaven, forgive me!), baby sitting on my knee,
I could close thy blue eyes calmly, smiling now so sweet on me!
Ay, *my* hand could ope the casket, and thy precious soul set free:
Better for thee death and heaven than a life of slavery!

—Mary A. Livermore, 1856[1]

People in mid-nineteenth-century society wondered whether "madness," badness, or a deep, abiding sadness had driven Margaret Garner to kill her child on that fated day. After all, it was not in the least typical for people to resist slavery by murder—especially murdering children. People concluded she suffered from some defect of soul, heart, or mind. Had Garner been driven by inherent evil, vindictiveness, impulsiveness, rebelliousness, or madness? Some historians and abolitionists consider infanticide/filicide an "extreme form" of reproductive resistance to slavery. Although it is an unsettling idea to some today, reproductive slave resistance sent powerful economic, political, and moral messages. If nothing else, it allowed enslaved women to take a direct blow at their owners' ability to profit from their offspring—thereby rejecting the commodification of their wombs. In addition, if the child was a product of rape, then that child's very existence may have represented a "dreadful threat to the entire Black family." A mother in that predicament may have believed that murdering that child would eliminate the threat to the family and the symbol of the mother's shame and degradation—a sort of erasure of trauma. Other women may have committed infanticide or filicide as a way to protest rape, and the rapists' power over their bodies and power to determine the paternity of their children. Reproductive resistance, then, could also send a message that enslaved women actually had the ultimate control over their bodies and reproductive capacity. Finally, women may have used these tactics to rescue their children from a lifetime of bondage.[2]

Those who committed reproductive resistance rarely killed living, breathing babies; even fewer killed older children. The two most common ways they committed reproductive resistance were by refusing to get pregnant at all or by terminating a pregnancy. The primary reason child murder never became a popular way to resist slavery is because mothers—even enslaved mothers—loved their children too much to risk losing them simply to send a message or seize a measure of power from their owners. The aching moral question that arises from this case is whether murder *is* indeed a form of resistance? If so, what type of murder counts as resistance? Most people today would agree that killing an innocent child is neither noble nor heroic. If Margaret had murdered as a form of resistance or a way to send a message to her owner, why had she not turned the knife toward Gaines or the deputies—the true embodiments of white male patriarchal power, instead? Little Mary, after all, was not a slave owner, and neither were the other Garner children.

Besides resistance, another possible reason Margaret Garner may have murdered her child is that she suffered from "madness," or mental illness. Today, people judge her for actions she committed in a historical racial-social context that few of us can imagine and with which even fewer can empathize. Mothers who committed infanticide shortly after childbirth in the mid-nineteenth century were believed to suffer from "puerperal insanity" or mania, or what today we know as postpartum depression. Mental health professionals today have arrived at a consensus about mothers who kill their children. They assert that the majority of murdering parents suffer from mental illness—whether post-traumatic stress disorder, postpartum depression, psychosis, or a psychotic illness, which might include schizo-phrenia, delusional or bipolar disorders, or severe depression. Apparently, too, the age of the children factors into the reasons these mothers kill. For example, mothers who kill a child within twenty-four hours of birth—neonaticide—typically are young women who are in denial about their pregnancies and kill their children out of fear of societal or parental scorn. Infanticide, the murder of a child one day old up to one year old, is typically committed by mothers suffering from postpartum depression. Filicide, or the murder of a child older than one, is not only exceedingly rare but typically a marker of psychosis, according to psychiatrists.[3]

Researchers have observed that parents who commit filicide act in specific ways. First, they tend to use weapons to complete the act; they also kill or attempt to kill multiple children, attempt suicide at the same time, and confess immediately thereafter. All factors were present in the Margaret Garner case. In recent psychological studies of filicide, psycho-sis is present in every single instance when a knife was used to murder a child. Moreover, researchers have determined that the use of weapons in an act of filicide is not related to the mother's anger, but is driven by their perceptions of the child's suffering or danger.[4] Margaret Garner defi-nitely believed her children were suffering. Another indicator for those who commit filicide is that the murderous parent harbors "acute feelings of failure to measure up to society's standards of 'good' mothers or wives."[5] Margaret's jarring words, "I have done the best I could!" echo here.[6]

Filicide can be typified in five categories: (1) altruistic filicide (mercy killing), (2) acutely psychotic filicide (driven by delusions or hallucina-tions), (3) unwanted child filicide (self-explanatory), (4) battering that leads to accidental filicide, and (5) spouse revenge filicide (in retaliation against a perceived rejection or wrongdoing by spouse).[7] Based on this rubric, Mary's death at her mother's hands best fits an altruistic filicide. Such murders are committed by a parent who believes he or she is sav-ing the child from "some real or imagined (often delusional, but not al-ways) condition, unbearable, inescapable torment or disease, or from the anticipated suffering from a parent's suicide." The parent truly loves the child, but believes it would be better off dead than experience the same existence as the parent.[8] Margaret Garner herself characterized her actions as a mercy killing. She used her own past suffering to predict the fate that awaited her children in the here and now, admitting that she was "unwilling to have her children suffer" as she had. She said, "I . . . would much rather kill them at once, and thus end their sufferings, than have them taken back to slavery and be murdered by piece meal."[9] In short, Garner asserted that her intention was simply to save her children from suffering in bondage. After Mary's death, Margaret expressed satisfaction that she had succeeded in freeing at least one of her children from slavery. Believing that little Mary had ascended into a better realm, she took some comfort that the babe was now "free from all trouble and sorrow." As if to underscore how much she believed the toddler had been freed from suffering, she referred to her as "the bird."[10] It is reasonable to conclude that psychosis can lead a mother—who by all evidence loved her child and understood the consequences of her actions—to filicide. Slavery, with all of its various traumas, certainly multiplied that possibility.

Within the framework of mercy killings, Mary's death could be considered a *gendered* mercy killing, and the attack on Cilla was also gendered. Margaret Garner made more decidedly deadly blows at her daughters. Had she singled out her daughters simply to save them from some uncertain unthinkable fate as enslaved women that included rape and bearing their rapist's children? That Mary—a girl and the one who was nearest to white of the four children—was attacked first and killed, may not have been a haphazard or random decision. Garner killed that babe so thoroughly too: accounts said that she nearly had been decapitated. Furthermore, Margaret was no less gentle with her other daughter, Cilla: she bashed her in the head with a coal shovel. It was such a hard blow that the infant's head swelled and blood ran from her nose. Her differentiated attacks on the girls illuminated how slavery despoiled the natural inviolability of mother-daughter bonds.

Although Garner also attacked her sons, they ended up with only superficial injuries, almost as if she did not truly want to kill them—perhaps because they were Robert's children? Or because they were boys? However, one could argue that the boys escaped worse fates because they were older and could run or fight back—which they did—while the girls were sitting targets because of their age, relative proximity, vulnerability, or inability to fight, run, or even know what was happening to them.

Yet, the fact that Garner's attacks on the girls were different from those on the boys underscores a differential relationship to her children based not only on gender, but possibly color, as well. Skin color may have had inverted importance to this enslaved woman. The girls' relatively lighter skin and the possibility that a white man fathered them may explain why she inflicted the most damage on them. Specifically, had she targeted her daughters because they were closer to white and she despised whiteness and all that it represented to her as an enslaved mother and wife? Were her blows then, an attack on whiteness . . . literally? If the girls were Gaines's daughters, perhaps her unparalleled brutality against them was a way to exact revenge on him? In a similar vein, had she done the most damage to these girls because they were a living reminder of her sexual abuse at his hands? This dialectic between love and loathing, protection and revenge as a possible reason that Garner targeted her daughters is heartbreaking.

Mental illness is socially determined. In other words, the behavior that can be classified as "mad" changes over place and time: how we define mental illness today is quite different than how it was defined in the seventeenth, eighteenth, or nineteenth centuries. In nineteenth-century psychology, "madness" was broadly used as a synonym for mental illness, insanity, hysteria, or extreme anger. When people acted with extreme rage, passion, emotion, or in ways that others could not easily rationalize, physicians quickly accused them of madness.

As it was socially constructed in 1856, mental illness was loaded with gendered meanings. Beginning in the nineteenth century, after decades of being associated with men, people began seeing it as a female affliction. This "feminization of madness" had consequences for women. For one, more women than ever before were labeled with madness—particularly, those who defied Victorian gender conventions. Victorian era gender conventions set a strict code of behavior for middle-class white women: they were expected to be caretakers of home and family, exclusively, while leaving politics, business, and law to men. Society severely condemned and scorned women who defied these expectations. Women were labeled "mad," "insane," "unwomanly," or "unnatural" for actions considered unmotherly, selfish, willful, violent, or overtly sexual. This label even extended to women who demanded such things as equality, a college education, the right to vote, or a job outside the home.[11]

Even if mental health professionals were just beginning to associate mental illness with women by the mid-1850s, very few associated it with African Americans. The label of madness as applied to African Americans was largely reserved for those who were free or who tried to secure their freedom. For example, a study published in 1851 in the *American Journal*

DRIVEN TOWARD MADNESS

of Insanity (later the *American Journal of Psychiatry*) observed an "amazing prevalence of insanity and idiocy among our free colored population" in the northern states. The study in the leading psychological journal of its day argued that freedom caused mental illness in African Americans.[12] This logic emerged from proslavery, racist arguments, which insisted that slavery civilized African Americans, and once freed, they degenerated into their "natural" states of depravity, immorality, and even mental illness. In the same vein, early psychological "research" found few instances of mental illness among enslaved African Americans and more instances of it among free blacks. These scholars concluded that freedom itself had led to a degeneracy of African Americans' mental health.

Samuel A. Cartwright, a physician writing in *DeBow's Review* in 1851, associated running away and everyday resistance to slavery with two distinct mental disorders, drapetomania (which literally translates to "mad runaway slave" in ancient Greek), which caused slaves to run away, and dysaesthesia aethiopica, which caused them to be troublesome as slaves. Drapetomania, he argued, was "as much a disease of the mind as any other species of mental alienation." The medical remedy for drapetomania, he advised, was adequate food and housing. If the condition persisted despite adequate nutrition and housing, the doctor advised slave owners to whip the afflicted slaves until they fell into a "submissive state." He concluded that dysaesthesia aethiopica was a blend of laziness and "rascality," which presented with the following symptoms:

> They [the slaves] break, waste and destroy everything they handle, —abuse horses and cattle,—tear, burn or rend their own clothing, and, paying no attention to the rights of property, steal others, to replace what they have destroyed. They wander about at night, and keep in a half nodding sleep during the day. They slight their work, —cut up corn, cane, cotton or tobacco when hoeing it, as if for pure mischief. They raise disturbances with their overseers and fellow-servants without cause or motive, and seem to be insensible to pain when subjected to punishment.[13]

The doctor also believed those afflicted with this mental illness could be cured by hard labor and whippings, which apparently sent "vitalized blood to the brain to give liberty to the mind." Dr. Cartwright basically categorized all manner of nonviolent slave resistance as mental illness. In other words, "badness" was linked to madness in African Americans, and madness was attached to those who desired freedom.[14] What this means is that because slavery was considered the natural state for African Americans, the psychological profession believed that any slave discontented with his or her status, who sought freedom by escape, and especially those who violently resisted slavery, was mad. Those who used violence in the process of escaping slavery categorically received the label of mad. For example, antebellum society pegged Nat Turner as a madman because he planned and executed a slave revolt in Southampton County, Virginia, in 1831, in which fifty-five whites were murdered.[15] It is in this historical context that Margaret Garner was accused of being "mad."

Even Garner's sympathizers were preoccupied with proving whether she had been driven by madness. Two ministers visited Margaret Garner in her jail cell shortly after her arrest. Ironically, both of these men of the cloth seemed more concerned with her sanity than the state of her soul. Reverend Horace Bushnell penned a strenuous defense of her sanity that was published in an abolitionist journal. His editorial seems in direct response to people's questions about Garner's sanity: "'But she was not deranged?' Not at all—calm, intelligent, but resolute and determined. 'But she was not fiendish, or beside herself with passion?' No, she was most tender and affectionate, and all her passion was that of a *mother's fondest love*." Reverend Bassett was perceptibly disgusted by the seeming satisfaction with which Margaret Garner spoke about Mary's death. He wrote, "She alludes to the child that she killed as being free from all trouble and sorrow, with a degree of satisfaction that almost chills the blood in one's veins."[16] This minister clearly could not sympathize with the state of mind of a woman who had spent her entire life in bondage and who had given birth to enslaved children with no hope of ever seeing them enjoy freedom.

Murdering a child and refusing to express remorse are not the only actions that led people to question Margaret Garner's sanity. Cilla's convenient drowning in the Ohio River and Margaret's odd reaction to it helped cement her image as a madwoman. People could not accept that fate alone had taken her second child—a child who miraculously had survived a blow to her face with a heavy shovel. People branded Margaret as a two-time child-killer. In its account of the details surrounding Cilla's drowning, the *Liberator* reported that Margaret "displayed frantic joy when told that her child was drowned." Moreover, the journal further printed that after Cilla's death, Garner declared that "she would never reach . . .

Gaines' Landing," implying that she intended to commit suicide.[17] Taken together, reports about Margaret's "joy" at Cilla's drowning, coupled with the alleged references to suicide, led people to conclude she was mad. The *Liberator* painted a particularly damning image of her: "The last that was seen of Peggy, she was on the *Hungarian,* crouching like a wild animal near the stove, with a blanket wrapped around her."[18] In short, even an abolitionist journal that was mostly sympathetic to African Americans succeeded in portraying Margaret Garner as a wild madwoman.

Although those affiliated with the case in 1856 generally believed Margaret Garner suffered from mental illness, she proclaimed her own sanity. When Reverend P. C. Bassett of the Fairmount Theological Seminary visited her in her cell in early February, he asked her point-blank if she had been "excited almost to madness" when she committed the act. She replied matter-of-factly, "No, I was as cool as I now am." In other words, Garner testified to her own sanity.[19] And because historians cannot prove her state of mind 150 years later, all we are left with is her own truth.

Tagging Garner with mental illness is as problematic now as it was then. By doing so, people then and now can avoid discussion of the ugly nature of slavery and the damage it did to African Americans' exteriors and interiors. Instead of critically examining the sadistic nature of slavery and the trauma it caused, it is easier to simply affix a label to Margaret and dismiss the conditions that led her to believe that filicide was her last best option. If we challenge the sexist, racist assumptions about madness in the antebellum era, Archibald K. Gaines, with his history of vicious and violent behavior, may be a better candidate for being considered mad.

The principal question always has been whether Margaret Garner was mad, but perhaps a better question is what madness defined her experience as an enslaved African American woman? In short, *what madness had driven her to kill?* Re-remembering that madness will expose the soul injuries she endured and why she could not bear to see her children suffer any longer. If we must insist that Margaret Garner's final act to achieve freedom is violently warped, twisted, and distorted, it is only because it is a mirror reflection of the slave experience that inspired it.

6   A KIND OF HERO

"Daughter," said he, "Virginia by your name,
There are two ways, for either death or shame
You now must suffer. Ah, that I was born!
For you have not deserved to be thus lorn,
To die by means of sword or any knife.
O my dear daughter, ender of my life,
Whom I have bred up with so deep pleasance
That you were never from my remembrance!
O daughter who are now my final woe,
Aye and in life my final joy also,
O gem of chastity, in patience
Receive your death, for that is my sentence.
For love and not for hate you must be dead;
My pitying hand must strike your head."

—Geoffrey Chaucer, circa 1387–1400[1]

The making of a hero begins when a real person does a courageous thing. Unfortunately, the real, historical people who made those difficult choices often get obscured by layers of convenient mythology that serve political ends. This is the case with Margaret Garner. Like everything else, our heroes are a product of our own historical, social, political, and economic conditions. They reflect the cultural values of their day. At times, how we define "hero" today is incongruent with how it was defined in an earlier moment in history. Our contemporary sensibilities cannot fathom how a mother could kill her child to save it from *anything*. Moreover, most of us would never consent to proclaiming a child-killer a hero—even if she had killed for seemingly noble reasons. To us today, Margaret Garner is simply a woman who behaved badly . . . or, better yet, madly. She is now considered a despicable woman—an antihero. Yet in the nineteenth century, activists such as Frederick Douglass to Lucy Stone to Harriet Beecher Stowe to Frances Ellen Watkins Harper respected her heroism. Margaret Garner, a fugitive slave woman who killed her daughter, is the first African American woman widely celebrated for heroic violent resistance to slavery in US history.[2] Examining why Margaret Garner became a hero and what kind of hero she became tells us much about nineteenth-century American society and African Americans' and women's political agency within it.

GARNER AS A CONVENIENT PROSLAVERY STEREOTYPE

Anytime a member of a marginalized, powerless group is hailed as a hero, an equally powerful counternarrative casts them as a villain. Vilification is, in fact, typical for those who use violence as the means of liberation. Nat Turner is the best example of that. So, too, are the Black Panthers in the twentieth century.

In response to the scrutiny of slavery and southern slaveholders in the northern press during the Garners' hearing, racist, proslavery minds constructed a complex set of overlapping stereotypes about Margaret Garner as a bad character, angry black woman, and bad mother. An anonymous editorial published in the *Covington Journal* 22 March 1856 and signed by "Justice," described her in the most vicious terms as "a very common cross tempered, flat nosed, thick-lipped negro woman, whose father was a very bad character." "Justice" focused on Garner's physical traits and her father's character to send readers the message that she not only was physically ugly—according to the white aesthetic, which denigrates thick lips and flat noses—but had inherited an ugliness of character to match. This linking of physical characteristics to bad character serves to reify the notion that this African American woman was naturally bad.[3]

The same editorial went on to posit that the "cross tempered" Garner had been driven to kill by "vexation and disappointment, arousing to a pitch of phrenzy a revengeful and devilish temper, inherited from her father." Other proslavery papers covering the story referred to her as "an infuriated negress." In other words, proslavery forces branded her as an angry black woman.[4]

Moreover, the same "Justice"—likely a neighbor and friend of Gaines—claimed that Margaret had been "cruel to her children at home" before the escape. In short, the editorial brands her with several overlapping and damning stereotypes as a bad woman and mother with a history of child abuse who was driven to filicide by an uncontrollable temper and vindictive nature.[5] Garner is one of the earliest embodiments of the angry (and violent) black woman stereotype in American history. Sadly, proslavery folks were not the only ones who perpetuated this mythology about Garner as an angry and violent black woman. In a private letter, Ohio governor and abolitionist Salmon Portland Chase concluded that she had a "naturally violent disposition."[6]

These efforts to cast Garner as the quintessential bad black woman belie reality and serve only to detract from the depravity of slavery and the conditions that had led her to flee and kill. Such stereotypes were created to negate the political import of Margaret's actions.

GARNER AS WOMEN'S RIGHTS SYMBOL

Even as proslavery advocates and Gaines's neighbors were busy trying to demonize Margaret Garner, Lucy Stone tried to use her as a symbol for women's rights. The construction of Margaret as a women's rights symbol within the abolitionist tradition began in earnest when Stone inserted herself into the case. She used her platform to expose the abuse suffered by enslaved women. Stone's courtroom address today would be considered a feminist act—even a *black* feminist act, because it addressed the intersectionalities of race, status, and gender, "sex and commerce, profit and power, economics and rape," and used black women's experiences as the basis of activism.[7]

Stone's public allegations about sexual abuse fall within the female abolitionist tradition, which centered on the sexual degradation of slave women. Women such as Harriet Beecher Stowe, Sarah Grimké, and Lydia Maria Child relied on stock archetypes of the sexually defiled slave woman and the traumatized slave mother whose children had been ripped from her and sold. Such archetypes allowed abolitionist women's rights advocates to indict slavery for its destruction of families and its degradation of women, while at the same time chastising slaveholders for violating Victorian values of pure womanhood. Writing and activism that focused on enslaved women's sexual and maternal trauma legitimized white women's political voice and made them authorities on southern slavery's impact on women.[8] Margaret Garner—cast as a sexually degraded woman and traumatized mother—conveniently embodied both messages.

In some ways, though, Lucy Stone diminished the women's movement by her decision to speak for Margaret Garner. Each time she told the story of her interaction with Garner, the details of the story changed, becoming decidedly more feminist each time. She may have had a compelling incentive to construct or embellish a narrative of Garner's alleged sexual abuse to advance her intersecting antislavery and women's rights agendas. Garner spoke to Stone in her cell in February 1856. Stone discussed that meeting at the close of the Garners' hearing. But when Stone spoke about the case at the American Antislavery Society meeting a few months later, she dramatized that conversation, creating a protofeminist caricature of Margaret Garner—similar to what Francis Dana Gage and Harriet Beecher Stowe later would do to Sojourner Truth. For example, in her embellished version, Margaret had pulled out a "sharpened dagger" to pour out the "life blood" of her daughter. Stone told her audience of abolitionists that Margaret needed to be guarded by six deputies, "lest by some desperate effort she should force her way from that crew and escape."[9] In other words, Margaret's herculean, superhuman strength and resolve to be free were so powerful that she was capable of overpowering six male deputies. Stone had inadvertently turned Garner into a caricature with superhuman physical strength.

Lucy Stone's daughter, Alice Stone Blackwell, wrote and published a biography of her activist mother in 1930, in which she briefly discusses the Garner case. In that book, she embellishes and falsifies the history to portray Margaret as a more deliberate feminist and to cast her actions as being more heroic than history allows. In Blackwell's version of the story, Margaret had "made sure" to kill Mary. She went on to claim that Margaret had vowed that "her daughter should never suffer as she had." The truth is that Margaret never admitted that she put more emphasis on killing the girls. She spoke only of wishing not to see her children suffer in general. These exaggerated words are better than the truth for this writer because they more concretely claim that Margaret had deliberately selected Mary to die and that she had killed her to prevent future sexual abuse. Blackwell continues the embellishment by writing that when her mother had addressed the court in February 1856, "the sweat of shame and anguish rolled down his [Gaines's] face." The sweat is a dramatization that suggests Gaines showed visible signs of guilt. None of the contemporary papers, even the antislavery *Cincinnati Daily Gazette*, commented on Gaines's sweat. Furthermore, in Blackwell's version of this history, Margaret had made "no effort" to save Cilla in that river, but had watched her child die. With this version of events, Blackwell implied that Margaret had committed a type of passive murder of her second daughter. Finally, Blackwell wrote that Margaret had died in a dramatic, watery suicide: "Margaret, refusing to be saved, allowed herself to drown, and thus attained freedom at last."[10] While trying to honor her mother's life, Blackwell's rendition of the Margaret Garner narrative had inadvertently endorsed the stereotype that she had been homicidally and suicidally, *mad*.

To African American women of her day, Margaret Garner became a commanding symbol of heroic or radical black womanhood. Frances Ellen Watkins Harper penned a poem about her. Locally, black women had vociferously stood in solidarity with Garner outside during her hearing. In the same spirit as Lucy Stone, black female abolitionist Sarah Parker Remond described the untenable burdens of enslaved black women to a British antislavery audience. She told that audience that Margaret "had suffered in her own person the degradation that a woman could not mention"—a clear reference to the alleged sexual abuse. Remond went on to explain that slave women, in general, could not "protect themselves from the licentiousness which met them on every hand" or "protect their honor from the tyrant." Remond framed Garner's actions as being a response to this type of abuse. Even thirty years later, black women still hailed Margaret Garner as their hero. Speaking at the inaugural meeting of the National Association of Colored Women in 1896, Rosetta Douglass Sprague, the daughter of abolitionist orator Frederick Douglass, named Margaret Garner in her list of history's greatest black women—a list that included Phillis Wheatley, Sojourner Truth, and Harriet Tubman.[11]

GARNER AS ABOLITIONIST HERO

Because they also assigned abolitionist political meaning to the murder she committed, abolitionists raised Margaret Garner as an antislavery hero. In his 27 May 1857 speech before the New England Anti-Slavery Convention, Wendell Phillips, one of the most progressive abolitionists who believed that black freedom should be accompanied by education and full equality, hailed Garner's actions as "heroic" and denounced Governor

Chase for allowing her to be remanded into slavery. Another abolitionist, Charles Lenox Remond of Salem, who is among the earliest of the black abolitionist orators, praised her in his 13 May 1858 speech before the Annual Meeting of the American Anti-Slavery Society in New York, stating that "a more heroic effort for freedom was never made by mortal man." Despite the hyperbole, Remond makes it abundantly clear that he respected Margaret's actions as antislavery, courageous, and heroic. In the same vein, the abolitionist black Canadian journal *Provincial Freeman* extolled her heroism and impact on history: "The name Margaret Garner shall live in the minds, and be cherished in the hearts of every true man and woman. . . . [She is] 'Unwept, unhonored, and unsung.'"[12] Although Margaret Garner had never spoken out against slavery in general, she became a potent symbol of the abolitionist movement.

Antebellum black abolitionists acknowledged and celebrated Margaret Garner among the pantheon of African Americans who waged deliberate, radical, and violent opposition to slavery. In fact, she is the only woman among a long list of male insurgents. Garner is America's first black female to be hailed as a hero of insurrectionary violence against slavery; never before had a woman been included among a group that until 1856 typically included Crispus Attucks, Denmark Vesey, Toussaint L'Ouverture, Gabriel Prosser, and Nat Turner. George T. Downing, in an 1860 letter to fellow black antislavery activist William Nell, mentions Margaret Garner in the same breath as black revolutionaries Crispus Attucks, Joseph Cinque, and black men who assisted John Brown in his 1859 raid on Harpers Ferry: Sheridan Lewis Leary (more popularly known as Lewis Sheridan Leary), John Anthony Copeland Jr., and Shields Green.[13] Frederick Douglass, himself a fugitive slave and abolitionist, speaking at the West India Emancipation in August 1857, hailed African Americans who spilled blood in the struggle for freedom:

> If we ever get free from the oppressions and wrongs heaped upon us, we must pay for their removal. We must do this by labor, by suffering, by sacrifice, and if needs be, by our lives and the lives of others. Hence, my friends, every mother who, like Margaret Garner, plunges a knife into the bosom of her infant to save it from the hell of our Christian Slavery, should be held and honored as a benefactress. Every fugitive from slavery who like the noble William Thomas at Wilkesbarre, prefers

to perish in a river made red by his own blood, to submission to the hell hounds who were hunting and shooting him, should be esteemed as a glorious martyr, worthy to be held in grateful memory by our people. The fugitive Horace, at Mechanicsburgh, Ohio, the other day, who taught the slave catchers from Kentucky that it was safer to arrest white men than to arrest him, did a most excellent service to our cause. Parker and his noble band of fifteen at Christiana, who defended themselves from the kidnappers with prayers and pistols, are entitled to the honor of making the first successful resistance to the Fugitive Slave Bill. . . . There was an important lesson in the conduct of that noble Krooman in New York, the other day, who, supposing that the American Christians were about to enslave him, betook himself to the mast head, and with knife in hand, said he would cut his throat before he would be made a slave. Joseph Cinque on the deck of the Amistad, did that which should make his name dear to us. He bore nature's burning protest against slavery. Madison Washington who struck down his oppressor on the deck of the Creole, is more worthy to be remembered than the colored man who shot Pitcairn at Bunker Hill.[14]

Here, Douglass highlights slaves who used violence to resist returning to bondage; the implication is that he believed this sort of violence was heroic, necessary, and worthy of martyrdom. Of all the people he mentions, Margaret Garner is the only female, underscoring how rare such actions were among women.[15]

Unlike those who used her as a symbol for their causes, the historical Margaret Garner had no overarching political philosophy; she planned no abolitionist activities and helped no one else escape from bondage. She came into her abolitionism through her own circumstances. Margaret Garner did not join a women's rights organization or speak on behalf of women as a group in any public forum. Yet her experiences made her acutely aware of black women's oppression in slavery—especially as mothers and wives. Although we cannot say that Margaret Garner espoused abolitionist or feminist philosophies, her actions are certainly abolitionist and feminist in deed. In a similar vein, Garner had not killed her daughter to send a political message about slavery. Her story reminds us that not all personal acts are intended to be political; some are simply personal acts done in public and become political through their weight. None of this should discount the political import of her actions, though, which proved to be a damning indictment of her slave experience and of her owner, in particular.

POSTSCRIPT

Fate was unkind to all parties central to this case. The Garner family was permanently separated after the hearing. Robert, Margaret, and their children were sent down the river, but Robert's parents remained in Boone County. It is not clear what happened to elder Simon, but Mary Garner was still at the Marshall farm in the 1860s. The younger family was further fractured once the Garners reached the Deep South. In New Orleans, Abner L. Gaines hired out the couple. He eventually sold the family to DeWitt Bonham, a probate judge in Issaquena County, Mississippi, who put them to work at his Willow Grove cotton plantation in Tennessee Landing, Mississippi. The last anyone heard of Margaret and Robert's eldest children, Tommy and Sammy, they were enslaved on a farm near Vicksburg, Mississippi. Their sibling, with whom Margaret was pregnant during the escape and subsequent hearing, disappeared from the historical record without a trace. Margaret Garner succumbed to typhoid fever just two years later, in 1858, at the tender age of twenty-five. According to Robert, before she died, she told him never again to marry as a slave, but to "live in hope of freedom."[1]

Of all the Garners, Robert left a more visible historical footprint after 1856. The Civil War provided opportunities for freedom for fugitive slaves who made it to Union lines. There, they could reasonably expect not to be returned to their owners. Robert, like so many other enslaved people, jettisoned his slave status. He made his way to Union lines and volunteered to serve the war effort like thousands of other formerly enslaved African

American men. He claimed to have cooked for the Union gunboat service on the Mississippi River aboard the USS *Benton* from June 1861 until October 1863. Garner's naval discharge papers do indeed attest to his Civil War service. He later claimed to have been shot just above his left knee during the siege of Vicksburg, leaving him disabled. Jolliffe, Robert's old attorney, assisted with his 1864 application for an Invalid Pension based on those claimed injuries. His claim was rejected though, for several reasons. First, the Navy claimed it had no record of his service: he is not listed on the official muster rolls for Mississippi or the *Official Records of the Union and Confederate Navies.* The second reason for his rejected pension claim is that according to the Bureau of Medicine and Surgery, Robert was not on the vessel's Register of the Sick and Wounded and, therefore, had no "disease or disability which . . . would entitle him to a pension." Finally, the bureau determined that "he had no serious illness, or disability originating in the line of duty." Robert's application for an Invalid Pension was duly rejected. Although it was common for African American men's Civil War pension claims to be rejected ostensibly for these same reasons, there is also a possibility that Garner had filed a false or exaggerated injury claim.[2]

After the war, Robert, then a free man and remarried, resettled in the Walnut Hills area of Cincinnati. Robert Garner became something of a living legend in the city—often asked to give speeches about his escape, the murder, and the fugitive slave hearing. People who saw him lecture remarked that he had prematurely aged. Decades after the escape, when he finally could openly defend the character of the wife of his youth, Robert insisted that Margaret had not drowned Cilla—contrary to what most people believed. He offered that she never again had attempted to kill any of their children. He made his living working on steamboats and as a plasterer. Similar to his previous pension application, Robert claimed to have received career-ending injuries when his ribs were broken while working on the steamer *Robert Burns.* He unsuccessfully sued the owners of the vessel for those injuries. Given his previous claim of a disabling war injury to his left leg, this second disability lawsuit highly suggests that Robert Garner may have made a career of filing spurious injury claims. That question, like so many others in this case, will remain a big question mark. He died from tuberculosis on 20 April 1871 at the age of forty-three. Ironically, Archibald K. Gaines died of tetanus on 11 November of the same year, after stepping on a rusty nail.[3] Their deaths finally ended this tragedy on the Ohio River.

NOTES

INTRODUCTION

1. bell hooks, "Healing Our Wounds: Liberatory Mental Health Care," in *Killing Rage: Ending Racism* (New York: Henry Holt, 1995), 142, 144; Nell Irvin Painter, "Soul Murder & Slavery: Toward a Fully Loaded Cost Accounting," in *Southern History across the Color Line* (Chapel Hill: University of North Carolina Press, 2002), 17; Debra Walker King, *African Americans and the Culture of Pain* (Charlottesville: University of Virginia Press, 2008), 37, 39, 169n1.

2. Wilma King, "'Mad' Enough to Kill: Enslaved Women, Murder, and Southern Courts," *Journal of African American History* 92, no. 1, "Women, Slavery, and Historical Research" (Winter 2007): 38.

3. Stephanie M. H. Camp, *Closer to Freedom: Enslaved Women and Everyday Resistance in the Plantation South* (Chapel Hill: University of North Carolina Press, 2004), 66–68.

4. Patricia Hill Collins, *Black Feminist Thought: Knowledge, Consciousness, and the Politics of Empowerment* (New York: Routledge, 1990), 50.

5. Steven Weisenburger, *Modern Medea: A Family Story of Slavery and Child-Murder from the Old South* (New York: Hill and Wang, 1998), 21.

6. Andrew J. Huebner, "Writing History with Emotion," *American Historian*, no. 1 (August 2014): 14–15.

CHAPTER 1: "HOPE FLED"

1. Frances Ellen Watkins Harper, "The Slave Mother, a Tale of the Ohio," 1857. Poem printed in its entirety in Mark Reinhardt, *Who Speaks for Margaret Garner?* (Minneapolis: University of Minnesota Press, 2010), 248–51.

2. John Hope Franklin and Loren Schweninger, *Runaway Slaves: Rebels on the Plantation, 1790–1860* (New York: Oxford University, 1999), 65–66.

3. Deborah Gray White, *Ar'n't I a Woman? Females Slaves in the Plantation South* (New York: W. W. Norton, 1985), 70–73.

4. Franklin and Schweninger, *Runaway Slaves*, 210, 212; Stephanie M. H. Camp, *Closer to Freedom: Enslaved Women and Everyday Resistance in the Plantation South* (Chapel Hill: University of North Carolina Press, 2004), 28–30, 36–37; *Cincinnati Daily Enquirer*, 31 January 1856; *Cincinnati Daily Gazette*, 1 and 2 February 1856.

5. Bernie D. Jones, "Southern Free Women of Color in the Antebellum North: Race, Class, and a 'New Women's Legal History,'" *Akron Law Review* 41, no. 3 (2008):

797; Elizabeth Fox-Genovese, *Within the Plantation Household: Black and White Women of the Old South* (Chapel Hill: University of North Carolina Press, 1988), 165–66.

6. Franklin and Schweninger, *Runaway Slaves*, 62, 64.

7. The four Kentucky slave revolts include one in 1810 in Lexington, one in Boone County in 1838, and two in 1848 in Fayette and Woodford Counties. Apparently, whites aided the one in Boone County. See Herbert Aptheker, *American Negro Slave Revolts* (New York: International Publishers, 1943), 248, 331, 338. The most violent revolt involving Kentucky slaves happened in 1826, when seventy-five people being transported from their homes in Bourbon County, Kentucky, to the Deep South killed five white men onboard a flatboat; University of Kentucky Libraries, Notable Kentucky African Americans Database, http://nkaa.uky.edu/subject.php?sub_id=87 (accessed 26 May 2016).

8. Harold D. Tallant, *Evil Necessity: Slavery and Political Culture in Antebellum Kentucky* (Lexington: University Press of Kentucky, 2003), 65, 69.

9. United States Census (Slave Schedule), 1850, Kentucky, Boone County Schedule 2, District no. 2, http://boonecountyky.us/slave-schedules-1850--g-h.htm#G1850 (accessed 9 June 2016).), Mary Adams (Washington, DC).

10. *Cincinnati Daily Enquirer*, 31 January 1856; *Cincinnati Daily Gazette*, 7 February 1856.

11. *Cincinnati Daily Enquirer*, 29 January and 1 February 1856; *Frankfort Commonwealth*, 5 February 1856.

12. United States Census Bureau, *The Seventh Census of the United States*, 1850 (Washington, DC: Robert Armstrong, 1853); *Cincinnati Daily Gazette*, 2 February 1856. *Cincinnati Daily Enquirer*, 29 January 1856.

13. For biographical information on Joseph Kite before arriving in Cincinnati, see Reverend Benjamin Arnett, *Proceedings of the Semi-Centenary Celebration of the African Methodist Episcopal Church of Cincinnati, held in Allen Temple, February 8th, 9th, and 10th, 1874* (Cincinnati: H. Watkin, 1874), 36; J. H. Woodruff, *The Cincinnati Directory and Advertiser for 1836–37* (Cincinnati: J. H. Woodruff, 1836); David Henry Shaffer, *The Cincinnati, Covington, Newport, and Fulton Directory for 1840* (Cincinnati: J. B. and R. P. Donogh Printers, 1839); Robinson and Jones, *Robinson and Jones' Cincinnati Directory for 1846* (Cincinnati: Robinson and Jones, 1846); United States Census Bureau, *Seventh Census*, 1850. The Kites' home on Sixth Street was valued at $1,300 in 1850, which today is equivalent to $40,700. For inflation calculator, see https://measuringworth.com/uscompare/relativevalue.php. If Joseph Kite had a trade, he would have been unable to utilize it because white laborers and employers were hostile to skilled African Americans and united to ensure that they were relegated to menial labor jobs instead. On the hostility to African American skilled workers in Cincinnati, see Nikki M. Taylor, *Frontiers of Freedom: Cincinnati's Black Community, 1802–1868* (Athens: Ohio University Press, 2005), 100–101. On the 1829 forced exodus, see Taylor, 50–65. For details of Elijah's escape, see Steven Weisenburger, *Modern Medea: A Family Story of Slavery and Child-Murder from the Old South* (New York: Hill and Wang, 1998), 69, 64, 69, 298n10; *Cincinnati Daily Gazette*, 2 February 1856.

14. Some sources name Elijah Kite's owner as William Harper. The 1850 census, though, includes a list of slave owners who lost slaves to escape during the year. That source indicates that three slaves escaped from a *Wilson* Harper from Boone County in 1850. Those slaves fit the age and gender profile of Elijah Kite, his young wife, and son.

15. *Cincinnati Daily Enquirer,* 3 February 1856; *Cincinnati Daily Gazette,* 2 February and 4 February 1856; Taylor, *Frontiers of Freedom,* 140; Stephen Middleton, *Black Laws: Race and the Legal Process in Early Ohio* (Athens: Ohio University Press, 2005), 177. For a complete narrative of the *State v. Farr* case, see Paul Finkelman, *An Imperfect Union: Slavery, Federalism, and Comity* (Chapel Hill: University of North Carolina Press, 1981), 165.

16. *Cincinnati Daily Enquirer,* 29 January 1856; *Cincinnati Daily Gazette,* 29 January 1856.

17. *Cincinnati Daily Enquirer,* 29 January 1856; *Cincinnati Daily Gazette,* 29 January 1856; *Anti-slavery Bugle* (New Lisbon, Ohio), 8 March 1856.

18. *Cincinnati Daily Enquirer,* 5 February 1856.

19. Although such an occurrence is extremely rare now, the Ohio River frequently froze over in the nineteenth century. Rutherford B. Hayes claimed that the river froze over in the winters of 1850, 1851, 1852, 1853, 1855, and 1856, which facilitated crossing on foot. See letter from "R. B. Hayes to Wilbur H. Siebert," Spring 1893, Wilbur H. Siebert Underground Railroad Collection: The Underground Railroad in Ohio: Hamilton County series IV, vol. 7; Levi Coffin, *Reminiscences of Levi Coffin, the Reputed President of the Underground Railroad; Being a Brief History of the Labors of a Lifetime in Behalf of the Slave, with the Stories of Numerous Fugitives, Who Gained Their Freedom Through His Instrumentality, and Many Other Incidents* (Cincinnati: Robert Clarke, 1880), 147, 471–72, http://docsouth.unc.edu/nc/coffin/coffin .html#p542 (accessed 19 February 2013); Harriet Beecher Stowe, *Uncle Tom's Cabin: Or Life among the Lowly* (Boston: John P. Jewett, 1852); available from https://nationalera .wordpress.com/table-of-contents/; Taylor, *Frontiers of Freedom,* 141.

20. Steven Weisenburger contends that the names Peggy and Simon were slave names that had been imposed on them by their owners (see Weisenburger, *Modern Medea,* 121). Both Reinhardt and Weisenburger seem to have overlooked the fact that Peggy is a common nickname for Margaret that she used most of her life until her escape. Reinhardt, *Who Speaks for Margaret Garner?,* 9, 12.

21. *Cincinnati Daily Enquirer,* 29 January 1856.

22. On the city's history of antiabolitionist violence, see Taylor, *Frontiers of Freedom,* 111–12, 123; *Daily Times,* 29 January 1856; Coffin, *Reminiscences,* 559.

23. *Daily Times,* 29 January 1856.

24. Paul Finkelman, "The Treason Trial of Castner Hanway," in *American Political Trials,* ed. Michal Belknap (Westport, CT: Greenwood Press, 1994), 81–83; Thomas D. Morris, *Free Men All: The Personal Liberty Laws of the North* (Baltimore: Johns Hopkins University Press, 1974), 130–47.

25. Finkelman, "Treason Trial of Castner Hanway," 83.

26. *Daily Times,* 28 January 1856; *Cincinnati Daily Chronicle,* 11 March 1870.

27. *Daily Times*, 28 January 1856.

28. *Daily Times*, 28 January 1856; *Cincinnati Daily Enquirer*, 29 and 30 January 1856.

29. General Assembly of the Commonwealth of Kentucky, *The Revised Statutes of Kentucky, Approved and Adopted by the General Assembly of 1851 and 1852 and in Force from July 1, 1852* (Cincinnati: Robert Clarke, 1860), 368, 375–76; Ivan E. McDougle, "Slavery in Kentucky, 1792–1865" (diss., Clark University, Worcester, MA, 1918), 38. For an example of white responses to black armed resistance in Cincinnati, see Taylor, *Frontiers of Freedom*, 117–26.

30. *Cincinnati Daily Enquirer*, 29 and 30 January 1856; *Daily Times*, 29 January 1856; *Cincinnati Daily Gazette*, 29 and 30 January 1856; *Anti-slavery Bugle* (New Lisbon, Ohio), 8 March 1856; Hamilton County, Ohio: Indictment Papers for Margaret Garner in MSS: Joseph Cox, series 631 BV2226. Held at the [Ohio] State Archives, http://www.ohiomemory.org/cdm/ref/collection/p267401coll32/id/16328 (accessed 12 February 2015). Sources have conflicting information about where Mary was found when authorities entered the Kite residence. The *Daily Times* reported that Mary was found wrapped in a quilt on a bed in a back room, while other sources claim she was found on the floor (without a quilt) of the front room.

31. *Daily Times*, 28 January 1856; *Cincinnati Daily Commercial*, 29 and 30 January 1856; *Liberator*, 21 March 1856; *Cincinnati Daily Gazette*, 29 January 1856; *Cincinnati Daily Enquirer*, 29 January 1856; *Commonwealth Frankfort*, 5 February 1856; *Weekly Indiana State Sentinel*, 7 February 1856. Also see Stephen Middleton, "The Fugitive Slave Crisis in Cincinnati, 1850–60," *Journal of Negro History* 72 (Winter–Spring 1987): 28. The details of the murder can be found in Weisenburger, *Modern Medea*, 62–75 passim. Weisenburger includes a summary on page 73.

32. Cathy Caruth, *Unclaimed Experience: Trauma, Narrative, and History* (Baltimore: Johns Hopkins University Press, 1996), 6, 17, 22–23, 91.

33. Sara Clarke Kaplan, "Love and Violence/Maternity and Death: Black Feminism and the Politics of Reading (Un)representability," *Black Women, Gender + Families* 1, no. 1 (Spring 2001): 96, 105.

34. *Daily Times*, 29 January 1856; *Cincinnati Daily Gazette*, 29 January 1856; *Anti-slavery Bugle* (New Lisbon, Ohio), 8 March 1856. One newspaper reported that the man who held her as she died was named Sutton; another said his name was Murphy (likely W. B. Murphy, who had been with the slaveholder's party the day of the capture).

35. John W. Menzies to John Pollard Gaines, 10 January, n.d., John Pollard Gaines Papers, at New York State Library, microfilm 979.503 G142, reel 2, p. 0291.

36. *Cincinnati Daily Enquirer*, 29 and 30 January 1856; *Cincinnati Daily Gazette*, 29 January 1856; *Daily Times*, 29 January 1856; *Covington Journal*, 22 March 1856.

CHAPTER 2: BEFORE THE BLOOD

1. Frances Ellen Watkins Harper, "The Slave Mother, a Tale of the Ohio," 1857. Poem printed in its entirety in Mark Reinhardt, *Who Speaks for Margaret Garner?* (Minneapolis: University of Minnesota Press, 2010), 248–51.

2. Robert William Fogel, *With Consent or Contract: The Rise and Fall of American Slavery* (New York: W. W. Norton, 1994), 36.

3. Harold D. Tallant, *Evil Necessity: Slavery and Political Culture in Antebellum Kentucky* (Lexington: University Press of Kentucky, 2003), 8; Lowell Hayes Harrison, *A New History of Kentucky* (Lexington: University Press of Kentucky, 1997), 135, 138; Asa Earl Martin, *The Anti-slavery Movement in Kentucky Prior to 1850* (Louisville: Standard Printing, 1918), 9.

4. Paul Turner, "Slavery in Boone County, Kentucky (and Its Aftermath)" (n.p., 1986), 7, http://bcplfusion.bcpl.org/Repository/slavery_boone_county_ky.pdf (accessed 22 August 2014).

5. On the definition of yeomen, see Elizabeth Fox-Genovese, *Within the Plantation Household: Black and White Women of the Old South* (Chapel Hill: University of North Carolina Press, 1988), 86; United States Census (Slave Schedule), 1850, Kentucky, Boone County, http://boonecountyky.us/slave-schedules-1850--g-h .htm#G1850 (accessed 9 July 2016), Mary Adams (Washington, DC); Turner, "Slavery in Boone County, Kentucky," 4; Reinhardt, *Who Speaks for Margaret Garner?*, 10.

6. *Cincinnati Daily Enquirer*, 29 January, 13 and 14 February 1856; *National Anti-Slavery Standard*, 15 March 1856; *Frankfort Commonwealth*, 12 February 1856; Tallant, *Evil Necessity*, 63.

7. Wilma King, "The Mistress and Her Maids: White and Black Women in a Louisiana Household, 1858–1868," in *Discovering the Women in Slavery: Emancipating Perspectives on the American Past*, ed. Patricia Morton (Athens: University of Georgia Press, 1996), 84.

8. Tallant, *Evil Necessity*, 63–66.

9. Steven Weisenburger, *Modern Medea: A Family Story of Slavery and Child-Murder from the Old South* (New York: Hill and Wang, 1998), 24. The Will of Abner Gaines, January 1839, cited in Ruth Wade Cox Brunings, "Modern Medea: Factual Errors" (n.p., n.d.); *Boone County Deed Book Q*, 1 May 1850; Elizabeth Coomer, "Gaines Tavern" (2006), http://www.nkyviews.com/boone/pdf/Gaines_Tavern_Coomer.pdf (accessed 22 November 2014), 5, 7, 8, 9.

10. Gaines Family Bible, "Collins and Gaines Family Bibles," transcribed copy, Genealogical Department of the Dallas Public, Dallas, TX. The only extant records of this family are in the John Pollard Gaines Papers at the New York State Library. Much of the material in those papers is related to John Pollard Gaines's service as governor and representative; very little is related to Maplewood or Gaines's slaves.

11. *Cincinnati Daily Gazette*, 11 and 12 February 1856; *New York Daily Tribune*, 16 February 1856; Reinhardt, *Who Speaks for Margaret Garner?*, 11; *US Agricultural and Manufacturing Census Records for Fifteen Southern States for the Year of 1850*, Boone County, Kentucky, District 2, p. 323, line 25, reel 31; Robert Patrick Bender, ed., *Worthy of the Cause for Which They Fought: The Civil War Diary of Brigadier General Daniel Harris Reynolds, 1861–1865* (Fayetteville: University of Arkansas Press, 2011), 196; Weisenburger, *Modern Medea*, 24; Coomer, "Gaines Tavern," 6; "Captain Danley's Statement," in John Pollard Gaines Papers, New York State Library, microfilm 979.503 G142, reel 3, p. 0058. Later published accounts of what happened to John P.

Gaines during that war claim he was *captured* by the Mexican military, not that he surrendered. See, for example, Clarence Wharton, *Texas under Many Flags* (Chicago: American Historical Society, 1930), 3:243.

12. *1830 United States Federal Census,* Ancestry.com (accessed 12 October 2014).

13. National Archives and Records Administration, *Record of Appointments of Postmasters, 1832–Sept. 30, 1971,* roll 4, M 841.

14. Gaines Family Bible, "Collins and Gaines Family Bibles," transcribed copy, Genealogical Department of the Dallas Public Library, Dallas, TX.; Wharton, *Texas under Many Flags,* 3:243.

15. Elizabeth's deathbed request might seem to suggest that she did not trust Archibald K. Gaines with their daughter. Deeper insight challenges that supposition, though. Nineteenth-century gender conventions dictated that men did not raise children alone. Many men had no idea how to do so. Besides that, people believed that only a woman could properly raise a female child. Consequently, dying mothers in that era often asked their mother, sister, or other female relatives to care for their children—especially for their daughters, so such a request was not unusual; Ruth Wade Cox Brunings, "Margaret Garner," http://boonecountykyhistory.org/pages/--margaret-garner---boone-county-slave.php (accessed 10 October 2014); Bender, 196.

16. *Cincinnati Daily Gazette,* 11 and 12 February 1856; *New York Daily Tribune,* 16 February 1856; Reinhardt, *Who Speaks for Margaret Garner?,* 11; Brunings, "Margaret Garner" (accessed 10 October 2014). There was some dispute at the hearing about whether John formally sold the bondspeople to his brother, Archibald. Regardless, Kentucky laws dictated that after five years, any informal sale became a bona fide sale.

17. Bertram Wyatt-Brown, *Southern Honor: Ethics & Behavior in the Old South* (New York: Oxford University Press, 2007), 219, 220; Heather Andrea Williams, *Help Me to Find My People: The African American Search for Family Lost in Slavery* (Chapel Hill: University of North Carolina Press, 2012), 61.

18. Historians have offered conflicting reports about the size of the Maplewood farm. The 1850 agricultural census indicates that farm was 210 acres. *US Agricultural and Manufacturing Census Records for Fifteen Southern States for the Year of 1850,* Boone County, Kentucky, District 2, p. 323, line 25, reel 31.

19. Ibid., p. 325, line 25, reel 31.

20. Ibid. Calculator at http://www.measuringworth.com/uscompare/relativevalue .php. For an early discussion of the economic concept of "prestige value," see Lindley M. Keasbey, "Prestige Value," *Quarterly Journal of Economics* 17, no. 3 (May 1903): 460–61.

21. Stephanie M. H. Camp, *Closer to Freedom: Enslaved Women and Everyday Resistance in the Plantation South* (Chapel Hill: University of North Carolina Press, 2004), 68.

22. Turner, "Slavery in Boone County, Kentucky," 13; United States Census (Slave Schedule), 1850, Kentucky, Boone County, http://boonecountyky.us/slave-schedules -1850--g-h.htm#G1850 (accessed 9 June 2016), Mary Adams (Washington, DC). Only twenty-three families in Boone County owned twelve or more bondspeople in 1850. United States Census (Slave Schedule), 1850.

23. Wyatt-Brown, *Southern Honor*, 14, 34, 35, 43, 46; Ariela J. Gross, *Double Character: Slavery and Mastery in the Antebellum Southern Courtroom* (Athens: University of Georgia, 2006), 47.

24. Wyatt-Brown, *Southern Honor*, 46–47, 88, 89; *Cincinnati Daily Gazette*, 11 February and 29 February 1856.

25. Wyatt-Brown, *Southern Honor*, 48–49; *Cincinnati Daily Gazette*, 11 February 1856.

26. Abner LeGrand Gaines to John Pollard Gaines, 12 September 1851, John Pollard Gaines Papers, New York State Library, microfilm 979.503 G142, reel 2, p. 0065.

27. United States Census Bureau, *The Seventh Census of the United States, 1850* (Washington, DC: Robert Armstrong, 1853).

28. *US Agricultural and Manufacturing Census Records for Fifteen Southern States for the Year of 1850*, Boone County, Kentucky, District 2, p. 323, line 34, reel 31.

29. Douglas R. Egerton, *Gabriel's Rebellion: The Virginia Slave Conspiracies of 1800 & 1802* (Chapel Hill: University of North Carolina Press, 1993), 24, 25.

30. John J. Zaborney, *Slaves for Hire: Renting Enslaved Laborers in Antebellum Virginia* (Baton Rouge: Louisiana State University Press, 2012), 1, 12–14 passim, 48; Egerton, *Gabriel's Rebellion*, 24.

31. *Cincinnati Daily Enquirer*, 5 February 1856.

32. Williams, *Help Me to Find My People*, 52, 53.

33. Rickie Solinger, *Pregnancy and Power: A Short History of Reproductive Politics in America* (New York: New York University Press, 2005), 16.

34. *Cincinnati Daily Gazette*, 11 February 1856.

35. "Wombs" are not to be confused with "breeders"; there are nuanced differences between them despite the fact that the net effect of both is new enslaved laborers. The term "breeder" implies white interference with slave women's reproduction, whereas "womb" implies a woman who has high fecundity naturally. For a definition of "breeder" see Dwight N. Hopkins, "Enslaved Black Women: A Theology of Justice and Reparations," in *Beyond Slavery: Overcoming Its Religious and Sexual Legacies*, ed. Bernadette J. Brooten (New York: Palgrave Macmillan, 2010), 294.

36. *Cincinnati Daily Gazette*, 1 February 1856; *Cincinnati Daily Enquirer*, 5 February 1856.

37. Various people had conflicting testimony about how long the elder Simon had been away from Richwood—some estimates given were seventeen, twenty, twenty-four, and twenty-five years. Both Mary Garner and James Marshall testified that Simon had been gone twenty-five years. Their recollections—as his wife and owner, respectively, would be more accurate. *Cincinnati Daily Enquirer*, 5 February 1856; *National Anti-Slavery Standard*, 15 March 1856.

38. All of the previous accounts about this case written by Weisenburger, Reinhardt, and Frederickson and Walters erroneously report that Robert was one year younger than Margaret. He, in fact, was five years her senior. Two government documents indicate he had been born in 1828. See "Form of Declaration for a Navy Invalid," 22 June 1864, in *Navy Survivors' Pension Files (Disapproved): Robert Garner*, file in online database at Fold3.com, http://www.fold3.com/image/1/274252583/ (accessed 23 November 2014) and *Hamilton County Death Records: 1870–73, Vol. II, Book A* (Cincinnati: Archives & Rare Books Department).

39. *Cincinnati Daily Gazette,* 11 February 1856; *New York Tribune,* 16 February 1856. On Margaret's paternity, see Weisenburger, *Modern Medea,* 32.

40. Abner L. Gaines to John Pollard Gaines, 1 October 1846, John Pollard Gaines Papers, New York State Library, microfilm 979.503 G142, reel 2. For a slaveholder's characterization of Margaret Garner's father, see *Covington Journal,* 22 March 1856.

41. Weisenburger and Reinhardt claim Margaret Garner's father's name was Duke. I never have found even one reference to that name in primary sources. On the use of the name Duke, see Weisenburger, *Modern Medea,* 20, 33, and Reinhardt, *Who Speaks for Margaret Garner?,* 13.

42. *Covington Journal,* 22 March 1856.

43. *Cincinnati Daily Enquirer,* 31 January 1856.

44. *Cincinnati Daily Gazette,* 11 February 1856; Robert/Simon Jr. was described in "Form of Declaration for a Navy Invalid," 22 June 1864, in *Navy Survivors' Pension Files (Disapproved): Robert Garner,* file in online database at Fold3.com, http://www .fold3.com/image/1/274252583 (accessed 23 November 2014). Margaret/Peggy was described in a biography of Lucy Stone; see Elinor Rice Hays, *Morning Star: A Biography of Lucy Stone, 1818–1893* (New York: Octagon Books, 1978), 140.

45. Emily West, *Chains of Love: Slave Couples in Antebellum South Carolina* (Urbana: University of Illinois Press, 2004), 54; Williams, *Help Me to Find My People,* 61.

46. Whitsuntide is mentioned in the *Cincinnati Daily Enquirer,* 5 February 1856. Whitsuntide is the seventh Sunday after Easter and commemorates the appearance of the Holy Spirit after Ascension. Slaves got these days off; *Cincinnati Daily Enquirer,* 31 January 1856.

47. Gwendolyn Tippie, "Afro-American Births of Boone through Bourbon County, 1852–61" (n.p. 1980), 7; *Cincinnati Daily Gazette,* 11 February 1856; Reinhardt, *Who Speaks for Margaret Garner?,* 11.

48. Marie Jenkins Schwartz, *Birthing a Slave: Motherhood and Medicine in the Antebellum South* (Cambridge, MA: Harvard University Press, 2006), 68.

49. Wilma King, *Stolen Childhood: Slave Youth in Nineteenth-Century America* (Bloomington: Indiana University Press, 1995), 6.

50. Marie Jenkins Schwartz, *Born in Bondage: Growing Up Enslaved in the Antebellum South* (Cambridge, MA: Harvard University Press, 2000), 65, 72.

51. *Liberator,* 16 May 1856; Wilbur H. Siebert Underground Railroad Collection: The Underground Railroad in Ohio: Hamilton County series IV, vol. 7, box 56.

52. Deborah Gray White, *Ar'n't I a Woman? Females Slaves in the Plantation South* (New York: W. W. Norton, 1985), 124–41 passim; Fox-Genovese, *Within the Plantation Household,* 18.

53. In 1855, an enslaved woman named Margaret was baptized at the Richwood Presbyterian Church (on the baptism of a woman of color, see *Richwood Session, Book II,* March 1855, 14. Also quoted in Reinhardt, *Who Speaks for Margaret Garner?,* 13 and Mary E. Frederickson and Delores M. Walters, eds., *Gendered Resistance: Women, Slavery, and the Legacy of Margaret Garner* [Champaign: University of Illinois Press, 2013], 18n2). If this Margaret was indeed Peggy Garner, it makes sense that she would use her formal or Christian name, Margaret, in a baptism ceremony. Of course, too, there is a higher possibility that *that* Margaret in the church records is *not* Margaret

Garner. After all, there were 2,100 African Americans in the county, and Margaret was a fairly common name at the time.

54. Edward Baptist, "The Absent Subject: African American Masculinity and Forced Migration to the Antebellum Plantation Frontier," in *Southern Manhood: Perspectives on Masculinity in the Old South,* ed. Craig Thompson Friend and Lorri Glover (Athens: University of Georgia Press, 2004), 137.

55. Daniel Black, *Dismantling Black Manhood: An Historical and Literary Analysis of the Legacy of Slavery* (New York: Garland Publishing, 1997), 100–101, 110, 112; *New Orleans Republican,* 16 March 1870.

56. Fay A. Yarbrough, "Power, Perception, and Interracial Sex: Former Slaves Recall a Multiracial South," *Journal of Southern History* 17, no. 3 (August 2005): 568; Eugene D. Genovese, *Roll, Jordan, Roll: The World the Slaves Made* (New York: Vintage Books, 1974), 490–91.

57. *National Anti-Slavery Standard,* 15 March 1856.

58. *Cincinnati Daily Enquirer,* 31 January 1856; Wilbur H. Siebert Underground Railroad Collection: The Underground Railroad in Ohio: Hamilton County series IV, vol. 7, box 56; Black, *Dismantling Black Manhood,* 120; Williams, *Help Me to Find My People,* 53, 57.

59. Baptist, "Absent Subject," 137; Black, *Dismantling Black Manhood,* 113, 124, 126; Herbert G. Gutman, *The Black Family in Slavery and Freedom, 1750–1925* (New York: Vintage Books, 1977), 264.

60. For more on how planning escapes instilled black men with manly confidence, see Baptist, "Absent Subject," 155.

CHAPTER 3: AFTER THE BLOOD

1. James M. Bell, excerpt from "Liberty or Death," *Provincial Freeman,* 8 March 1856.

2. "Perils of Escape Told by Allen Sidney," *Detroit Sunday News Tribune,* 12 August 1894, in Wilbur H. Siebert Underground Railroad Collection: The Underground Railroad in Ohio: Hamilton County series IV, vol. 7, boxes 106 and 107; "Testimony of Henry Young" in Wilbur H. Siebert Underground Railroad Collection: The Underground Railroad in Ohio: Hamilton County series IV, vol. 7, box 56; Laura Haviland, *A Woman's Life-Work: Labors and Experiences of Laura S. Haviland* (Chicago: Publishing Association of Friends, 1889), 166, 167, https://catalog.hathitrust .org/Record/009834508; Levi Coffin, *Reminiscences of Levi Coffin, the Reputed President of the Underground Railroad; Being a Brief History of the Labors of a Lifetime in Behalf of the Slave, with the Stories of Numerous Fugitives, Who Gained Their Freedom Through His Instrumentality, and Many Other Incidents* (Cincinnati: Robert Clarke, 1880), 308–9, 330–32, 335, 347, http://docsouth.unc.edu/nc/coffin/coffin.html#p542 (accessed 19 February 2013); Wilbur Henry Siebert, *The Mysteries of Ohio's Underground Railroads* (Columbus, OH: Long's College Book Company, 1951), 32; Rev. Calvin Fairbank, *Rev. Calvin Fairbank during Slavery Times: How He "Fought the Good Fight" to Prepare "The Way"* (Chicago: R. R. McCabe, 1890), 35, 60; "Glorious Old Thief," *Chicago Tribune,* 29 January 1893, in Wilbur H. Siebert Underground Railroad Collection: The Underground Railroad in Ohio: Hamilton County series

IV, vol. 7, boxes 106, 107. Young must have mistakenly called John Hatfield, James. There was no James Hatfield in Cincinnati.

3. Fairbank, *During Slavery Times*, 21, 60.

4. Transcript of interview of "Ex-Pres R. B. Hayes," Spring 1893, in Wilbur H. Siebert Underground Railroad Collection: The Underground Railroad in Ohio: Hamilton County series IV, vol. 7, boxes 106, 107.

5. Nikki M. Taylor, *Frontiers of Freedom: Cincinnati's Black Community, 1802–1868* (Athens: Ohio University Press, 2005), 4–7 passim; Richard Wade, *The Urban Frontier: The Rise of Western Cities, 1790–1830* (Cambridge, MA: Harvard University Press, 1959), 22.

6. *Miller v. McQuerry*, 17 Fed. Cas. 335 (CCD Ohio, 1853), also reported in 10 *Western Law Journal* 528 (1853). This case is also discussed in Coffin, *Reminiscences*, 542–48 passim.

7. *Cincinnati Daily Gazette*, 17 August 1853; *Cincinnati Daily Enquirer*, 17 August 1853; *Cincinnati Daily Commercial*, 18 August 1853; Coffin, *Reminiscences*, 545.

8. Coffin, *Reminiscences*, 546, 547.

9. Ibid., 549–51.

10. Taylor, *Frontiers of Freedom*, 118.

11. Coffin, *Reminiscences*, 554–57; Paul Finkelman, *An Imperfect Union: Slavery, Federalism, and Comity* (Union, NJ: Lawbook Exchange, 2000), 175–76.

12. *Cincinnati Daily Gazette*, 29 January 1856.

13. *Cincinnati Daily Enquirer*, 29 and 30 January 1856; *Daily Courier* (Louisville), 1 February 1856; *Daily Times*, 29 January 1856; *Cincinnati Daily Gazette*, 30 January 1856; *Daily Cleveland Herald*, 31 January 1856.

14. *Cincinnati Daily Gazette*, 29 January and 1 February 1856; *Louisville Courier*, 30 January 1856; *Daily Cleveland Herald*, 31 January 1856.

15. *Daily Times*, 29 January 1856; *Daily Courier* (Louisville), 1 February 1856.

16. The word "Confederacy" here simply means co-conspirators. The word was in use before the birth of the Confederate States of America. *Daily Times*, 29 January 1856; *Cincinnati Daily Gazette*, 30 January 1856.

17. All the major Cincinnati papers covered the hearing, although some did in greater detail or more objectively than others. *Cincinnati Daily Enquirer*, for example, was the most detailed, but also the most biased of all the newspapers.

18. *Daily Times*, 31 January 1856; *Daily Enquirer*, 31 January 1856; *Cincinnati Daily Gazette*, 1 February 1856.

19. Steven Weisenburger, *Modern Medea: A Family Story of Slavery and Child-Murder from the Old South* (New York: Hill and Wang, 1998), 92–93.

20. Stephen Middleton, *Black Laws: Race and the Legal Process in Early Ohio* (Athens: Ohio University Press, 2005), 177.

21. *Cincinnati Daily Gazette*, 1 February 1856; *Cincinnati Daily Enquirer*, 31 January 1856; Frankfort *Commonwealth*, 19 February 1856.

22. *Cincinnati Daily Gazette*, 1 February 1856.

23. Ibid.; Mark Reinhardt, *Who Speaks for Margaret Garner?* (Minneapolis: University of Minnesota Press, 2010), 73–74.

24. *Daily Times,* 31 January 1856; Reinhardt, *Who Speaks for Margaret Garner?,* 276.

25. *Cincinnati Daily Gazette,* 1 February 1856; Reinhardt, *Who Speaks for Margaret Garner?,* 277.

26. *Cincinnati Daily Gazette,* 1 February 1856.

27. Mark Reinhardt contends that the white community knew the couple as Peggy and Simon, and the black community knew them as Margaret and Robert. He posits that the aliases are proof of naming resistance on Peggy and Simon's part (see Reinhardt, *Who Speaks for Margaret Garner?,* 9, 12). Both Reinhardt and Weisenburger seem to have overlooked the fact that Peggy is a common nickname for Margaret that she used most of her life until her escape. Hence, it is too strong to suggest that her using the name Margaret was naming resistance. Enslaved people who resisted names imposed on them by their owners would be known by whites as one thing, and by African Americans as another. However, in this case, the white Richwood community and the Garners' relatives *all* knew the couple by the names Peggy and Simon. For example, when Archibald K. Gaines reported on slave births as was required by law after 1852, he reported that "Peggy" gave birth to Mary on 16 August 1853 (see Tippie, "Afro-American Births," 7). Even more telling is that Peggy's free black relatives, Sarah Kite and her son, Elijah, used the name "Young Simon" in their court testimonies to refer to Robert (see reference in *Cincinnati Daily Gazette,* 4 February 1856). Hence, both communities used these same names. Just because the names Peggy and Simon were nicknames and not slave names, as these scholars suggest, does not mean we should diminish the power or efficacy of their assuming their formal names in freedom. On the practice of renaming, see Lois E. Horton, *Harriet Tubman and the Fight for Freedom: A Brief History with Documents* (Boston: Bedford/St. Martin's, 2013), 31.

28. *Cincinnati Daily Enquirer,* 1 February 1856; *Kentucky State Flag,* 6 February 1856.

29. *Cincinnati Daily Gazette,* 2, 3, and 4 February 1856; *Cincinnati Daily Enquirer,* 3 and 5 February 1856; *New York Tribune,* 16 February 1856; *Louisville Democrat,* 1 February 1856.

30. *New York Tribune,* 16 February 1856; *Cincinnati Daily Enquirer,* 8 February 1856; *Cincinnati Daily Gazette,* 7 February 1856; *Anti-slavery Bugle,* 8 March 1856. Paul Finkelman, "The Supreme Court and Slavery in the 1850s," *Race, Racism and the Law,* http://racism.org/index.php?option=com_content&view=article&id=1518 :supremecourtslavery&catid=119&Itemid=243 (accessed 30 May 2016).

31. *Cincinnati Daily Gazette,* 7 February 1856; *Cincinnati Daily Enquirer,* 8 February 1856; *Anti-slavery Bugle,* 8 March 1856; *Frankfort Commonwealth,* 1 February 1856.

32. Hamilton County, Ohio: Indictment Papers for Margaret Garner in MSS: Joseph Cox, series 631 BV2226. Held at the [Ohio] State Archives. http://www .ohiomemory.org/cdm/ref/collection/p267401coll32/id/16328 (accessed 12 February 2015); *Cincinnati Daily Enquirer,* 8 and 9 February 1856; *Cincinnati Daily Gazette,* 8 February 1856.

33. *Cincinnati Daily Gazette,* 11 February 1856.

34. Ibid.

35. *Daily Courier* (Louisville), 30 January 1856; also reprinted in its entirety in Reinhardt, *Who Speaks for Margaret Garner?*, 53–57; *Cincinnati Daily Gazette*, 11 February 1856.

36. *Cincinnati Daily Gazette*, 11 February 1856. For a definition of "disenfranchised grief," see Kenneth J. Doka, *Disenfranchised Grief: Recognizing Hidden Sorrow* (New York: Lexington Books, 1989), 4; Heather Andrea Williams, *Help Me to Find My People: The African American Search for Family Lost in Slavery* (Chapel Hill: University of North Carolina Press, 2012), 88.

37. *Cincinnati Daily Gazette*, 11 and 12 February 1856; *Cincinnati Daily Enquirer*, 13 February 1856; *New York Tribune*, 16 February 1856; *Kentucky State Flag*, 6 February 1856.

38. Ohio Anti-Slavery Society, *Proceedings of the Ohio Anti-Slavery Society Convention, Putnam 22–24 April 1836* (Beaumont and Wallace, 1836), in Wilbur H. Siebert Underground Railroad Collection: The Underground Railroad in Ohio: Hamilton County series IV, vol. 10, box 59; *Liberator*, 16 May 1856; Wilbur H. Siebert Underground Railroad Collection: The Underground Railroad in Ohio: Hamilton County series IV, vol. 7, box 56.

39. Kristine Yohe, "Enslaved Women's Resistance and Survival Strategies in Frances Ellen Watkins Harper's 'The Slave Mother: A Tale of the Ohio' and Toni Morrison's *Beloved* and Margaret Garner," in *Gendered Resistance: Women, Slavery, and the Legacy of Margaret Garner*, ed. Mary E. Frederickson and Delores M. Walters (Champaign: University of Illinois Press, 2013), 103–4.

40. John Hope Franklin and Loren Schweninger, *Runaway Slaves: Rebels on the Plantation, 1790–1860* (New York: Oxford University Press, 1999), 52–53.

41. Harold D. Tallant, *Evil Necessity: Slavery and Political Culture in Antebellum Kentucky* (Lexington: University Press of Kentucky, 2003), 64; Robert William Fogel, *Without Consent or Contract: The Rise and Fall of American Slavery* (New York: W. W. Norton, 1994), 152.

42. For the concept of the "perpetually suspended death sentence," see Sara Clarke Kaplan, "Love and Violence/Maternity and Death: Black Feminism and the Politics of Reading (Un)representability," *Black Women, Gender + Families* 1, no. 1 (Spring 2001): 95.

43. *National Anti-Slavery Standard*, 15 March 1856; *Liberator*, 16 May 1856.

44. *Cincinnati Daily Gazette*, 29 January 1856; *National Anti-Slavery Standard*, 15 March 1856.

45. Joelle Million, *Woman's Voice, Woman's Place: Lucy Stone and the Birth of the Woman's Rights Movement* (Westport, CT: Praeger, 2003), 191–92.

46. *National Era*, 28 February 1856.

47. *Cincinnati Daily Gazette*, 14 February 1856.

48. Only the *Gazette* mentioned the phrase about faded faces. The *National Era* carefully reported Stone's words verbatim that day, but did not mention the part about the "faded faces," and neither did the *Daily Scioto Gazette* (Chillicothe, Ohio) or *Covington Journal*. For Stone's speech, see *Cincinnati Daily Gazette*, 14 February 1856; *Daily Scioto Gazette*, 26 February 1856; *Covington Journal*, 16 February 1856; and *National Era*, 28 February 1856. One could argue that the journals

omitted the phrase to protect honor itself. Another possibility is that reporters for those journals were not in the courtroom that day and relied on less reliable eye-witnesses. Finally, there is the possibility that the *Gazette* had fabricated that part of Stone's statement.

49. *Cincinnati Daily Gazette*, 14 February 1856; *National Era*, 28 February 1856; *Daily Scioto Gazette*, 26 February 1856. Also quoted in Elinor Rice Hays, *Morning Star: A Biography of Lucy Stone, 1818–1893* (New York: Octagon Books, 1978), 140–41.

50. Jennifer L. Griffiths, *Traumatic Possessions: The Body and Memory in African American Women's Writing and Performance* (Charlottesville: University of Virginia Press, 2010), 8.

51. Jane Kilby, *Violence and the Cultural Politics of Trauma* (Edinburgh: Edinburgh University Press, 2007), 34.

52. Judith Butler, *Undoing Gender* (New York: Routledge, 2004), 155.

53. Elaine Scarry, *The Body in Pain: The Making and Unmaking of the World* (New York: Oxford University Press, 1985), 3; Mae G. Henderson, "Toni Morrison's *Beloved*: Re-Membering the Body as Historical Text," in *Toni Morrison's Beloved: A Casebook*, ed. William L. Andrews and Nellie Y. McKay (New York: Oxford University, 1999), 86; Lisa Woolfork, *Embodying American Slavery in Contemporary Culture* (Urbana: University of Illinois Press, 2009), 62.

54. Griffiths, *Traumatic Possessions*, 51.

55. *Cincinnati Daily Gazette*, 11 February 1856; *New York Daily Tribune*, 16 February 1856.

56. Carol E. Henderson, *Scarring the Black Body: Race and Representation in African American Literature* (Columbia: University of Missouri Press, 2002), 49; Mae G. Henderson, "Toni Morrison's *Beloved*," 87; Hortense J. Spillers makes a distinction between the body and flesh. She uses the term "flesh" to discuss enslaved people, and "body" in reference to free people. Hortense J. Spillers, "Mama's Baby, Papa's Maybe: An American Grammar Book," in *African American Literary Theory: A Reader*, ed. Winston Napier (New York: New York University Press, 2000), 260; Woolfork, *Embodying American Slavery*, 61; Deborah E. McDowell, "Recovery Missions: Imagining the Body Ideals," in *Recovering the Black Female Body: Self-Representations by African American Women*, ed. Michael Bennett and Vanessa D. Dickerson (New Brunswick, NJ: Rutgers University Press, 2001), 208–9.

57. Walter Johnson, *Soul by Soul: Life inside the Antebellum Slave Market* (Cambridge, MA: Harvard University Press, 1999), 145.

58. Fay A. Yarbrough, "Power, Perception, and Interracial Sex: Former Slaves Recall a Multiracial South," *Journal of Southern History* 17, no. 3 (August 2005): 568.

59. *National Anti-Slavery Standard*, 15 March 1856; *Daily Cleveland Herald*, 31 January 1856.

60. *National Anti-Slavery Standard*, 15 March 1856.

61. *Cincinnati Gazette*, 4 February 1856; *Cincinnati Daily Enquirer*, 3 February 1856.

62. *Daily Times*, 29 February, 1856.

63. *National Anti-Slavery Standard*, 15 March 1856.

64. Joshua D. Rothman, *Notorious in the Neighborhood: Sex and Families across the Color Line in Virginia, 1787–1861* (Chapel Hill: University of North Carolina Press, 2003), 138–39; Yarbrough, "Power, Perception, and Interracial Sex," 568; Kenneth M. Stampp, *The Peculiar Institution: Slavery in the Ante-Bellum South* (New York: Vintage Books, 1956), 359.

65. Henry Bibb, Narrative of the Life and Adventures of Henry Bibb, An American Slave, Written by Himself, 43–44. Electronic version http://docsouth.unc.edu /neh/bibb/bibb.html (accessed 2 June 2016).

66. Cathy Caruth, *Unclaimed Experience: Trauma, Narrative, and History* (Baltimore: Johns Hopkins University Press, 1996), 7; Kaplan, "Love and Violence/Maternity and Death," 95.

67. *Cincinnati Daily Gazette*, 27 February 1856; *Daily Times*, 29 February 1856.

68. Wilbur H. Siebert Underground Railroad Collection: The Underground Railroad in Ohio: Hamilton County series IV, vol. 7; *Daily Gazette*, 29 February 1856; *Daily Times*, 29 February 1856.

69. *Cincinnati Daily Gazette*, 27 February 1856; *Daily Times*, 29 February 1856; *Anti-slavery Bugle* (New Lisbon, Ohio), 8 March 1856.

70. *Cincinnati Daily Gazette*, 29 February 1856; *Cincinnati Columbian*, 29 February 1856, cited in Wilbur H. Siebert Underground Railroad Collection: The Underground Railroad in Ohio: Hamilton County series IV, vol. 7, box 56; Reinhardt, *Who Speaks for Margaret Garner?*, 279.

71. *Liberator*, 2 May 1856; Joseph Cox to Salmon P. Chase, *Indictment*, 15 May 1856, in Joseph Cox MSS at the Ohio State Archives series 631 BV2226. Held at the [Ohio] State Archives, http://www.ohiomemory.org/cdm/ref/collection /p267401coll32/id/16328 (accessed 12 February 2015); Reinhardt, *Who Speaks for Margaret Garner?*, 280.

72. *Liberator*, 21 March 1856; Reinhardt, *Who Speaks for Margaret Garner?*, 126.

73. *Liberator*, 21 March 1856; *Cincinnati Daily Commercial*, 12 March 1856; Wilbur H. Siebert Underground Railroad Collection: The Underground Railroad in Ohio: Hamilton County series IV, vol. 7, box 56.

74. *Liberator*, 21 March 1856; *Cincinnati Daily Commercial*, 12 March 1856.

75. *Cincinnati Daily Enquirer*, 15 April 1856; *Liberator*, 2 May 1856; *National Anti-Slavery Standard*, 13 June 1857, in Reinhardt, *Who Speaks for Margaret Garner?*, 232–34.

76. *Cincinnati Gazette*, quoted in Samuel May, *The Fugitive Slave Law and Its Victims* (New York: National Anti-Slavery Society, 1861), 60; *Liberator*, 2 May 1856.

77. Ariela J. Gross, *Double Character: Slavery and Mastery in the Antebellum Southern Courtroom* (Athens: University of Georgia Press, 2006), 50.

78. Ibid., 47.

79. *Cincinnati Daily Enquirer*, 15 April 1856.

80. *National Anti-Slavery Standard*, 13 June 1857.

81. Taylor, *Frontiers of Freedom*, 111–12; James Oliver Horton and Lois E. Horton, *In Hope of Liberty: Culture, Community and Protest among Northern Free Blacks, 1700–1860* (New York: Oxford University Press, 1997), 240.

82. *National Anti-Slavery Standard*, 13 June 1857; *Cincinnati Daily Enquirer*, 15 April 1856; *Liberator*, 2 May 1856; Bertram Wyatt-Brown, *Southern Honor: Ethics & Behavior in the Old South* (New York: Oxford University Press, 2007), 374–75.

CHAPTER 4: "FADED FACES" TELL SECRETS—OR DO THEY?

1. Elizabeth Barrett Browning, "The Runaway at Pilgrim's Point" (1848).

2. *Cincinnati Daily Gazette*, 14 February 1856.

3. Alice Stone Blackwell, *Lucy Stone: Pioneer of Woman's Rights* (Boston: Little, Brown, 1930), 184.

4. Although the historical record does not definitively state that Margaret Garner was raped by her owner, Archibald K. Gaines, contemporaries and scholars implied it, using euphemisms of distraction. The scholar Anthony W. Neal asks why historians are reluctant to use the word "rape" in describing sexual encounters between slaveholders and their bondswomen. He accuses scholars of "mask[ing] the slaveholder's brutal takeover of the bondswoman's body by using various obfuscatory words and phrases such as philandering, finding pleasure, prostitution, procuring sexual favors, seduction, sexual experimentation, miscegenation, and making love." The author of a monograph about the Margaret Garner tragedy proves Neal correct in his observation. Steven Weisenburger, author of *Modern Medea*, did not include the word "rape" in his index even once. Instead, he uses the more cumbersome "miscegenation," which is not only anachronistic, but not necessarily about rape. One of the handful of times Weisenburger uses the word "rape," on page 48, he quickly adds, "of course the power differential was always there, but it could be turned to a variety of advantages." So, for him, the power differential that favored the rapist could be mitigated by the "advantages"—or perks—that the survivor might receive. It is dangerous to suggest that rape was a part of a transaction that is equivalent to prostitution or even concubinage. In addition, Weisenburger uses the concept of "fathering" as yet another euphemism for rape: for him, Gaines merely "fathered" Garner's children. As a result, scholars have avoided a robust discussion of the threat and realities of rape that enslaved women endured. The failure to utter the word "rape" as it relates to this case denies a reality that enslaved women faced in general, and Margaret Garner, specifically. Anthony W. Neal, *Unburdened by Conscience: A Black People's Account of America's Ante-bellum South and the Aftermath* (Lanham, MD: University Press of America, 2010), 52; Steven Weisenburger, *Modern Medea: A Family Story of Slavery and Child-Murder from the Old South* (New York: Hill and Wang, 1998), 48, 157, 175.

5. Sharon Block, *Rape and Sexual Power in Early America* (Chapel Hill: University of North Carolina Press, 2006), 67.

6. Ibid., 29, 64; Julie A. Allison and Lawrence S. Wrightsman, *Rape: The Misunderstood Crime* (Newbury Park, CA: Sage Publications, 1993), 198.

7. Fay A. Yarbrough, "Power, Perception, and Interracial Sex: Former Slaves Recall a Multiracial South," *Journal of Southern History* 17, no. 3 (August 2005): 565; Peter Kolchin, *American Slavery, 1619–1877* (New York: Hill and Wang, 1993), 124, 125; Block, *Rape and Sexual Power*, 66.

8. Catherine Clinton, "Breaking the Silence: Sexual Hypocrisies from Thomas Jefferson to Strom Thurmond," in *Beyond Slavery: Overcoming Its Religious and Sexual Legacies*, ed. Bernadette J. Brooten (New York: Palgrave Macmillan, 2010), 215.

9. Diane Miller Sommerville, *Rape & Race in the Nineteenth-Century South* (Chapel Hill: University of North Carolina Press, 2004), 148.

10. Ibid., 64–65; Peter W. Bardaglio, "Rape and Law in the Old South: 'Calculated to Excite Indignation in Every Heart,'" *Journal of Southern History* 60, no. 4 (November 1995): 756, 757.

11. Sharon Block discovered that not one white man was convicted of raping an enslaved woman between 1700 and the Civil War. Block, *Rape and Sexual Power*, 65.

12. Ibid., 65, 66, 86; Deborah Gray White, *Ar'n't I a Woman? Females Slaves in the Plantation South* (New York: W. W. Norton, 1985), 78; Estelle B. Freedman, *Redefining Rape: Sexual Violence in the Era of Suffrage and Segregation* (Cambridge, MA: Harvard University Press, 2013), 4; Neal, *Unburdened by Conscience*, 51; Joshua D. Rothman, *Notorious in the Neighborhood: Sex and Families across the Color Line in Virginia, 1787–1861* (Chapel Hill: University of North Carolina Press, 2003), 9; Dorothy Roberts, "The Paradox of Silence and Display: Sexual Violation of Enslaved Women and Contemporary Contradictions in Black Female Sexuality," in *Beyond Slavery: Overcoming Its Religious and Sexual Legacies*, ed. Bernadette J. Brooten (New York: Palgrave Macmillan, 2010), 43.

13. White, *Ar'n't I a Woman?*, 30–31, 38–39; Roberts, "Paradox of Silence and Display," 44–45; Fay Botham, "The 'Purity' of the White Woman, Not Purity of the Negro Woman: The Contemporary Legacies of Historical Laws against Interracial Marriage," in *Beyond Slavery: Overcoming Its Religious and Sexual Legacies*, ed. Bernadette J. Brooten (New York: Palgrave Macmillan, 2010), 254–55.

14. *Cincinnati Daily Enquirer*, 15 April 1856.

15. United States Census, 1850, Kentucky, Boone County Schedule 2, District no. 2, https://familysearch.org/pal:/MM9.1.1/MVHW-T16 (accessed 15 February 2013), Mary Adams (Washington, DC).

16. Thavolia Glymph, *Out of the House of Bondage: The Transformation of the Plantation Household* (Cambridge: Cambridge University Press, 2008), 35. Glymph challenges the consensus that slave-owning women (mistresses) were not key actors in the violence of slave management. Such a view, she insists, diminishes the agency and power these women actually had. Glymph refutes the idea that the violence these women committed was impulsive.

17. Allison and Wrightsman, *Rape: The Misunderstood Crime*, 27–33; Ann Wolbert Burgess and Lynda Lytle Holmstrom, "Rape Trauma Syndrome and Post Traumatic Stress Response," in *Rape and Sexual Assault: A Research Handbook*, ed. Ann Wolbert Burgess (New York: Garland, 1985), 49.

18. Block, *Rape and Sexual Power*, 181.

19. Neal, *Unburdened by Conscience*, 62; Louisa Picquet, *Louisa Picquet, the Octoroon; or, Inside Views of Southern Domestic Life* (New York: H. Mattison, 1861), 14, 15, http://docsouth.unc.edu/neh/picquet/picquet.html (accessed 12 September 2013).

20. Weisenburger, *Modern Medea*, 40–41.

21. Rothman, *Notorious in the Neighborhood*, 134; *Cincinnati Daily Gazette*, 29 February 1856; *Cincinnati Columbian*, 29 February 1856, cited in Wilbur H. Siebert Underground Railroad Collection: The Underground Railroad in Ohio: Hamilton County series IV, vol. 7, box 56.

22. Annette Gordon-Reed, *Thomas Jefferson and Sally Hemings: An American Controversy* (Charlottesville: University of Virginia Press, 1997), xix.

23. Legal historian Annette Gordon-Reed reminded us that in the eighteenth and nineteenth centuries, paternity was established by proving the putative father had access to the mother of the child at the time of conception. Through meticulous research about Thomas Jefferson's comings and goings at Monticello, Gordon-Reed established that Jefferson had access to Sally Hemings at the time of her conception and, therefore, likely fathered her children. Gordon-Reid, *Thomas Jefferson and Sally Hemings*, 98–99.

24. Steven Weisenburger lists the birth dates of the children as March 1850, 1852, May 1853, and April 1855. Weisenburger, *Modern Medea*, 45. Mark Reinhardt refers to a Gaines family Bible in the possession of Gaines's descendants, which purportedly lists the birth dates of the Garner children as 21 April 1851, 29 March 1854, and September 1856. A common practice in American families was to record family genealogy in Bibles. Reinhardt never has seen the Bible alleged to contain these dates because the Gaines descendants hold the Bible under lock and key. A photocopy of the Bible is in the Dallas Public Library, but it does not include any mention of Margaret Garner or her children. Because the actual evidence attesting to the dates of birth of the Garner children never has been seen by a historian or validated by a source outside of the Gaines family, these birth dates are questionable. Moreover, it would be highly unusual for a slave-owning family to include the birth dates of its enslaved workforce in its family Bible alongside its own genealogy—unless of course, those family trees were one and the same. So in their futile efforts to disprove Weisenburger's claims that Margaret Garner conceived her children during the final months of Archibald's wife's pregnancies, the Gaines descendants refer to the damning evidence that Margaret's children were, in fact, part of the Gaines family tree. Mark Reinhardt, *Who Speaks for Margaret Garner?* (Minneapolis: University of Minnesota Press, 2010), 292n30.

25. *Cincinnati Daily Commercial*, 30 January 1856; *Cincinnati Daily Enquirer*, 31 January and 12 February 1856; *Cincinnati Daily Gazette*, 11 and 27 February 1856; *New York Tribune*, 16 February 1856. Another source that draws on local newspaper accounts describes Margaret as a "dark mulatto" and little Mary as "nearly white." See "Anti-Slavery Tracts No 15," in Wilbur H. Siebert Underground Railroad Collection: The Underground Railroad in Ohio: Hamilton County series IV, vol. 7, box 56.

26. Ian Hanley Lopez, *White by Law: The Legal Construction of Race* (New York: New York University Press, 2006), 83.

27. Ariela J. Gross, "Litigating Whiteness: Trials of Racial Determination in the Nineteenth-Century South," *Yale Law Journal* 108, no. 1 (October 1998): 122, 130, 137.

28. Ibid.; *Cincinnati Daily Gazette*, 11 February 1856.

29. I use the term "race-mixing" because according to Evelynn M. Hammonds and Rebecca M. Herzig, the word "miscegenation" did not enter the American

lexicon until 1863. Evelynn M. Hammonds and Rebecca M. Herzig, *The Nature of Difference: Sciences of Race in the United State from Jefferson to Genomics* (Cambridge, MA: MIT Press, 2008), 238.

30. Now skin tone can be scientifically measured using a spectrophotometer, or reflectometer.

31. For skin color, scientists use an instrument called the reflectance spectroscope on the upper inner arm to calculate a modified melanin (MM) index.

32. Richard A. Sturm, Neil F. Box, and Michele Ramsay, "Human Pigmentation Genetics: The Difference Is Only Skin Deep," *Bioessays* 20 (1998): 712–13; Nina G. Jablonski, *Living Color: The Biological and Social Meaning of Skin Color* (Berkeley: University of California Press, 2012), 65–66.

33. Srirupa Banerjee, "Polygenic Inheritance" (March 2012), http://www.dna2life .com/polygenic-inheritance (accessed 9 August 2014); Frank W. Sweet, "The Heredity of Racial Traits: Essays on the Color Line and the One-Drop Rule," *Essays on the U.S. Color Line,* December 2004, http://essays.backintyme.biz/item11 (accessed 10 August 2014); Frank W. Sweet, *Legal History of the Color Line: The Rise and Triumph of the One-Drop Rule* (Palm Coast, FL: Backintyme, 2005), 42.

34. Sweet, *Legal History of the Color Line,* 42–43.

35. Technically, there is no way she could have been "one-third white" since fractions of blood are divisible by twos—not threes—because people have two parents, four grandparents, and so forth. *Cincinnati Daily Gazette,* 11 February 1856. Described in Elinor Rice Hays, *Morning Star: A Biography of Lucy Stone, 1818–1893* (New York: Octagon Books, 1978), 140.

36. Gregory S. Barsh, "What Controls Variation in Human Skin Color?" *PloS Biology,* 13 October 2003, http://www.ncbi.nlm.nih.gov/pmc/articles/PMC212702/ (accessed 24 February 2014); Lawrence R. Tenzer, "How Do We Inherit Our Skin Color?," *The Multiracial Activist,* October/November 2000, http://multiracial.com /site/content/view/459/27/ (accessed 24 March 2014); Robert/Simon Jr. was described in "Form of Declaration for a Navy Invalid," 22 June 1864, in *Navy Survivors' Pension Files (Disapproved): Robert Garner,* file in database at Fold3.com, http://www .fold3.com/image/1/274252583/ (accessed 23 November 2014); Margaret/Peggy was described in a biography of Stone: see Hays, *Morning Star,* 140.

37. Sweet, "Essays on the Color Line and One-Drop Rule"; Sweet, *Legal History of the Color Line,* 40, 42; Jablonski, *Living Color* 148; D. Y. Wang, "Skin Color, IQ, and Quantitative Inheritance," http://www.bio.miami.edu/dywang/skincoloriqquantative .html (accessed 21 May 2015).

38. For a Punnett Square calculator, see http://scienceprimer.com/punnett-square -calculator. This three-gene Punnett Square assumes that AABBCC genotypes possess the darkest possible skin, while aabbcc genotypes produce the lightest possible—or white—skin. A mixed person would be represented by the genotype AaBbCc. Margaret Garner, then, would be represented on the Punnett Square as AaBbCc, while Robert—possessing darker skin color genes than his wife—would be represented by one of the genotypes AABbCc, AaBBCc, AaBbCC, AABBCC, AABBcc, aaBBCC, AAbbCC, AABbCC, AaBBCC, or AABBCc, all of which produce medium brown to

dark skin. If we simply assume his genotype was AABbCc (slightly darker than Margaret), then there is zero possibility that he and Margaret could produce a phenotypically white child (aabbcc), only a 3.1 percent chance they could produce one with only slightly visible traces of melanin (Aabbcc), and only a 6.3 percent chance they could produce a child slightly darker than that (AabbCc, AaBbcc, aaBbcc, aabbCc, etc).

39. Sweet, *Legal History of the Color Line*, 50, 75. In other words, it would be exceedingly rare for two such parents to produce a child who was phenotypically as light as the Garner girls were described by observers.

40. Tenzer, "How Do We Inherit Our Skin Color?"

41. Dorothy E. Roberts, "The Genetic Tie," *University of Chicago Law Review* 62, no. 1 (Winter 1995): 260.

42. United States Census Bureau, *The Seventh Census of the United States*, 1850 (Washington, DC: Robert Armstrong, 1853), Boone County, Kentucky, District 2, p. 45; United States Census Bureau, *The Eighth Census of the United States*, 1860, Boone County, Kentucky, District 2, p. 4191; *Cincinnati Daily Gazette*, 12 February 1856; *New York Daily Tribune*, 16 February 1856.

43. *Cincinnati Daily Commercial*, 30 January 1856.

44. In *Modern Medea*, Steven Weisenburger claims that Gaines cried 'uncontrollably" over Mary's body and was babbling "incoherent phrases" about wanting to take her to Kentucky. Weisenburger also claims that the deputies had a "difficult time persuading the distraught" Gaines to release Mary's body. Unfortunately, the sources do not support this rather dramatic rendering of events, effectively discounting the more important point he made about Gaines's preoccupation with securing Mary's corpse. Weisenburger, *Modern Medea*, 75–76.

45. Ibid., 47.

46. On dissemblance see Darlene Clark Hine, "Rape and the Inner Lives of Black Women in the Middle West: Preliminary Thoughts on the Culture of Dissemblance," in *"We Specialize in the Wholly Impossible: A Reader in Black Women's History*, ed. Darlene Clark Hine, Wilma King, and Linda Reed (New York: Routledge, 1994), 342. On silence see Jane Kilby, *Violence and the Cultural Politics of Trauma* (Edinburgh: Edinburgh University Press, 2007), 3, and Cathy Winkler, *One Night: Realities of Rape* (Walnut Creek, CA: AltaMira Press, 2002), 287; Yarbrough, "Power, Perception, and Interracial Sex," 567.

47. Rothman, *Notorious in the Neighborhood*, 51; Bertram Wyatt-Brown, *Southern Honor: Ethics & Behavior in the Old South* (New York: Oxford University Press, 2007), 308.

48. White, *Ar'n't I a Woman?*, 40–43.

49. *New York Daily Tribune*, 16 February 1856.

50. Bertram Wyatt-Brown, *Honor and Violence in the Old South* (New York: Oxford University Press, 1986), 105, 106; Clinton, "Breaking the Silence," 218, 219.

51. *Cincinnati Daily Commercial*, 16 April 1856; *Liberator*, 2 May 1856.

52. Carolyn J. Powell, "In Remembrance of Mira: Reflections on the Death of a Slave Woman," in *Discovering the Women in Slavery: Emancipating Perspectives on the American Past*, ed. Patricia Morton (Athens: University of Georgia Press, 1996), 58.

53. Rothman, *Notorious in the Neighborhood*, 50, 51; Reinhardt, *Who Speaks for Margaret Garner?*, 31.

54. *Cincinnati Daily Enquirer*, 14 February 1856; *Covington Journal*, 22 March 1856.

55. On "transcendent silence," see Wyatt-Brown, *Southern Honor*, 308, 310; Powell, "In Remembrance of Mira," 52.

CHAPTER 5: DRIVEN BY MADNESS, BADNESS, OR SADNESS?

1. Mary A. Livermore, "The Slave Tragedy at Cincinnati." Originally in *New York Daily Tribune*, 9 February 1856. *Liberator*, 22 February 1856; poem also printed in its entirety in Mark Reinhardt, *Who Speaks for Margaret Garner?* (Minneapolis: University of Minnesota Press, 2010), 247–48.

2. Elizabeth Fox-Genovese, *Within the Plantation Household: Black and White Women of the Old South* (Chapel Hill: University of North Carolina Press, 1988), 324; Dorothy Roberts, *Killing the Black Body: Race, Reproduction, and the Meaning of Liberty* (New York: Vintage Books, 1997), 48–49. For other stories of infanticide, see Eugene D. Genovese, *Roll, Jordan, Roll: The World the Slaves Made* (New York: Vintage Books, 1974), 496–97; Deborah Gray White, *Ar'n't I a Woman? Females Slaves in the Plantation South* (New York: W. W. Norton, 1985), 87–89; Stephanie Shaw, "Mothering under Slavery in the Antebellum South," in *Mothers and Motherhood: Readings in American History*, ed. Janet Golden and Rima Apple (Columbus: Ohio State University Press, 1997), 309; Rickie Solinger, *Pregnancy and Power: A Short History of Reproductive Politics in America* (New York: New York University Press, 2005), 33.

3. On puerperal insanity, Wilma King, "'Mad' Enough to Kill: Enslaved Women, Murder, and Southern Courts," *Journal of African American History* 92, no. 1, *Women, Slavery, and Historical Research* (Winter 2007): 43. On contemporary mental illness see Stacey L. Shipley, "Perpetrators and Victims: Maternal Filicide and Mental Illness," in *It's A Crime: Women and Justice*, ed. Roslyn Muraskin (New York: Prentice Hall, 2000), 66, 69, 78.

4. Shipley, "Perpetrators and Victims," 83, 84, 85.

5. Ibid., 71.

6. *Liberator*, 16 May 1856; Wilbur H. Siebert Underground Railroad Collection: The Underground Railroad in Ohio: Hamilton County series IV, vol. 7, boxes 106, 107.

7. Shipley, "Perpetrators and Victims," 70–72.

8. Ibid., 69, 70–72.

9. *National Anti-Slavery Standard*, 15 March 1856.

10. Ibid. When someone complimented her on her sons' good looks, she said, "You should have seen my little girl that—that (she did not like to say—was killed)—that died, that was the bird." Although this statement was in reference to good looks, it is a double entendre, meaning Mary, the bird, flew away to freedom.

11. Anne Digby, *Madness, Morality, and Medicine: A Study of the York Retreat, 1796–1914* (Cambridge: Cambridge University Press, 1985), 17.

12. Anonymous, "Startling Facts from the Census," *American Journal of Insanity* 8, no. 2 (October 1851): 153–55.

13. Samuel A. Cartwright, "Diseases and Peculiarities of the Negro Race," in *DeBow's Review* (1851), http://www.pbs.org/wgbh/aia/part4/4h3106t.html (accessed 10 July 2014).

14. John Hope Franklin and Loren Schweninger, *Runaway Slaves: Rebels on the Plantation, 1790–1860* (New York: Oxford University Press, 1999), 275–75; Lauren J. Tenney, "Psychiatric Slave No More: Parallels to a Black Liberation Psychology," *Radical Psychology* 7 (2008), http://www.radicalpsychology.org/vol7-1/tenney2008.html (accessed 9 June 2016).

15. For contemporary portrayals of Nat Turner as a "fanatic" or "madman," see *Norfolk Herald,* 4 November 1831, and *Constitutional Whig,* 26 September 1831, in *The Confessions of Nat Turner and Related Documents,* ed. Kenneth S. Greenberg (Boston: Bedford/St. Martin's, 1996), 78–90.

16. *Liberator,* 16 May 1856; Wilbur H. Siebert Underground Railroad Collection: The Underground Railroad in Ohio: Hamilton County series IV, vol. 7, box 56; *National Anti-Slavery Standard,* 15 March 1856.

17. *Liberator,* 21 March 1856.

18. Ibid.

19. Wilbur H. Siebert Underground Railroad Collection: The Underground Railroad in Ohio: Hamilton County series IV, vol. 7, box 56.

CHAPTER 6: A KIND OF HERO

1. Geoffrey Chaucer, "The Physician's Tale," in *The Canterbury's Tales,* edited by Sinan Kökbugur (n.p., circa 1387), lines 213–26, http://www.librarius.com/canttran /phystale/phystale213-250.htm.

2. Also see Frederick Douglass's praises for her in his speech "West India Emancipation," delivered at Canandaigua, NY, 3 August 1857, which can be found at http://www.lib.rochester.edu/index.cfm?PAGE=4398.

3. *Covington Journal,* 22 March 1856.

4. *Daily Courier* (Louisville), 30 January 1856; Also reprinted in its entirety in Mark Reinhardt, *Who Speaks for Margaret Garner?* (Minneapolis: University of Minnesota Press, 2010), 53–57; *Covington Journal,* 22 March 1856; *Liberator,* 16 May 1856.

5. *Liberator,* 16 May 1856.

6. *Salmon Portland Chase to John T. Trowbridge,* 13 March 1864. Letter printed in Reinhardt, *Who Speaks for Margaret Garner?,* 139–42.

7. Veta Smith Tucker, "Secret Agents: Black Women Insurgents on Abolitionist Battlegrounds," in *Gendered Resistance: Women, Slavery, and the Legacy of Margaret Garner,* ed. Mary E. Frederickson and Delores M. Walters (Chicago: University of Illinois Press, 2013), 78. I am *not* saying that Lucy Stone was a black feminist, but that her *actions* on that particular day were because they embraced black feminist ideas such as intersectionality and placing lived experiences front and center. For a clearer definition of black feminism and a discussion of who might be considered a black feminist, see Patricia Hill Collins, *Black Feminist Thought: Knowledge, Consciousness, and the Politics of Empowerment* (New York: Routledge, 1990), chap. 2.

8. Franny Nudelman, "Harriet Jacobs and the Sentimental Politics of Female Suffering," *ELH* 59, no. 4 (Winter 1992): 940, 941, 943; Jennifer Fleischner, *Mastering*

Slavery: Memory, Family, and Identity in Women's Slave Narratives (New York: New York University Press, 1996), 37–38.

9. *Anti-slavery Bugle*, 25 May 1856.

10. Alice Stone Blackwell, *Lucy Stone: Pioneer of Woman's Rights* (Boston: Little, Brown, 1930), 184–85.

11. James Oliver Horton and Lois E. Horton, *In Hope of Liberty: Culture, Community and Protest among Northern Free Blacks, 1700–1860* (New York: Oxford University Press, 1997), 83; *Warrington Times*, 29 January 1859.

12. *Cincinnati Daily Enquirer*, 29 January 1856; *Liberator*, 5 June 1857. For Remond's speech in its entirety, see *Liberator*, 29 February 1856 and 21 May 1858; *Provincial Freeman*, 22 March 1856.

13. George T. Downing to William C. Nell, 3 March 1860, letter printed in *Liberator*, 16 March 1860.

14. Douglass, "West India Emancipation," 3 August 1857.

15. Sara Clarke Kaplan is absolutely wrong when she insists that Margaret Garner "was largely divorced from that of the heroic—if terrifying—insurgent male slaves." Kaplan, "Love and Violence/Maternity and Death: Black Feminism and the Politics of Reading (Un)representability," *Black Women, Gender + Families* 1, no. 1 (Spring 2001): 102.

Postscript

1. *New York Daily Tribune*, 22 September 1862; *Cincinnati Daily Chronicle*, 11 March 1870; Steven Weisenburger, *Modern Medea: A Family Story of Slavery and Child-Murder from the Old South* (New York: Hill and Wang, 1998), 243–45.

2. *Cincinnati Daily Chronicle*, 11 March 1870. On the lack of evidence of Garner's service on muster rolls, see Mississippi's muster rolls at http://teva.contentdm .oclc.org/cdm/ref/collection/p15138coll6/id/3468 (accessed 23 November 2014) and "Treasury Department letter," 23 August 1888, in *Navy Survivors' Pension Files (Disapproved): Robert Garner*, file in online database at Fold3.com, http://www.fold3.com /image/274252570/ (accessed 23 November 2014). Garner's name is also missing from the *Official Records of the Union and Confederate Navies*, online database at Fold3.com, http://www.fold3.com/image/313406266/ (accessed 23 November 2014). There is a Robert S. *Garnett* listed on those rolls, which could be his name, wrongly recorded as a result of someone misreading the handwriting in the original document, which was quite common. "Brief of Claim for Invalid Claim for Robert Garner," 12 October 1863, in *Navy Survivors' Pension Files (Disapproved): Robert Garner*, file in online database at Fold3.com, http://www.fold3.com/image/274252588/ (accessed 23 November 2014); "Form of Declaration for a Navy Invalid," 22 June 1864, in *Navy Survivors' Pension Files (Disapproved): Robert Garner*, file in Online database at Fold3.com, http://www.fold3 .com/image/1/274252583/ (accessed 23 November 2014); "Discharge," 12 October 1863, in *Navy Survivors' Pension Files (Disapproved): Robert Garner*, file in online database at Fold3.com, http://www.fold3.com/image/1/274252594/ (accessed 23 November 2014).

3. *Cincinnati Daily Chronicle*, 11 March 1870; *Cincinnati Daily Gazette*, 11 March 1870 and 4 January 1871; *Hamilton County Death Records: 1870–73, Vol. II, Book A* (Cincinnati: Prepared by the Archives & Rare Books Department, University of Cincinnati).

SELECTED BIBLIOGRAPHY

NEWSPAPERS

Anti-slavery Bugle
Carroll Free Press
Cincinnati Daily Chronicle
Cincinnati Daily Commercial
Cincinnati Daily Enquirer
Cincinnati Daily Gazette
Cleveland Morning Leader
Covington Journal
Daily Democrat
Daily Times
Daily Union
Eaton Democrat
Evansville Argus
Evansville Daily Journal
Frankfort Commonwealth
Holmes County Republican
Kentucky State Flag
Lexington Kentucky Statesman
Liberator
Louisville Democrat
Maysville Eagle
Meigs County Telegraph
Nashville Union and American
National Anti-Slavery Standard
National Era
New Orleans Republican
New York Daily Times
New York Daily Tribune
Provincial Freeman
Weekly Indiana State Sentinel
Wheeling Daily Intelligencer

Manuscript Collections

Joseph Cox Papers, series 631 BV2226. Held at the [Ohio] State Archives.

John Pollard Gaines Papers, at New York State Library, microfilm 979.503 G142.

Wilbur H. Siebert Underground Railroad Collection: The Underground Railroad in Ohio: Hamilton County. Held at the Ohio Historical Society Archives.

Government Records

United States Federal Census, 1840–70.

United States Census (Slave Schedule), 1850, Kentucky, Boone County.

United States Census (Slave Schedule), 1860, Kentucky, Boone County.

United States Agricultural and Manufacturing Census, 1840, 1850, 1860, 1870. Boone County, Kentucky.

Published Primary Sources

Arnett, Reverend Benjamin. *Proceedings of the Semi-Centenary Celebration of the African Methodist Episcopal Church of Cincinnati, held in Allen Temple, February 8th, 9th, and 10th, 1874.* Cincinnati: H. Watkin, 1874.

Coffin, Levi. *Reminiscences of Levi Coffin, the Reputed President of the Underground Railroad; Being a Brief History of the Labors of a Lifetime in Behalf of the Slave, with the Stories of Numerous Fugitives, Who Gained Their Freedom Through His Instrumentality, and Many Other Incidents.* Cincinnati: Robert Clarke, 1880.

Fairbank, Rev. Calvin. *Rev. Calvin Fairbank during Slavery Times: How He "Fought the Good Fight" to Prepare "The Way."* Chicago: R. R. McCabe, 1890.

Secondary Sources

Alexander, Adele Logan. *Homelands and Waterways: The American Journey of the Bond Family, 1846–1926.* New York: Pantheon, 1999.

Andrews, William L., and Nellie Y. McKay, eds. *Toni Morrison's Beloved: A Casebook.* New York: Oxford University Press, 1999.

Baptist, Edward E. "The Absent Subject: African American Masculinity and Forced Migration to the Antebellum Plantation Frontier." In *Southern Manhood: Perspectives on Masculinity in the Old South,* edited by Craig Thompson Friend and Lorri Glover, 136–73. Athens: University of Georgia Press, 2004.

———. "'Cuffy,' 'Fancy Maids,' and 'One-Eyed Men': Rape, Commodification, and the Domestic Slave Trade in the United States." *American Historical Review* 106, no. 5 (December 2001): 1619–50.

Bardaglio, Peter W. *Reconstructing the Household: Families, Sex, and the Law in the Nineteenth-Century South.* Chapel Hill: University of North Carolina Press, 1995.

Bender, Robert Patrick, ed. *Worthy of the Cause for Which They Fought: The Civil War Diary of Brigadier General Daniel Harris Reynolds, 1861–1865.* Fayetteville: University of Arkansas Press, 2011.

Bennett, Michael, and Vanessa D. Dickerson, eds. *Recovering the Black Female Body: Self-Representations by African American Women.* New Brunswick, NJ: Rutgers University Press, 2001.

Selected Bibliography

Berlin, Ira. *Many Thousands Gone: The First Two Centuries of Slavery in North America.* Cambridge, MA: Belknap Press of Harvard University Press, 1998.

Berry, Daina Ramey. *"Swing the Sickle for the Harvest Is Ripe": Gender and Slavery in Antebellum Georgia.* Urbana: University of Illinois Press, 2007.

Black, Daniel. *Dismantling Black Manhood: An Historical and Literary Analysis of the Legacy of Slavery.* New York: Garland Publishing, 1997.

Blackett, Richard J. M. *Beating against the Barriers: Biographical Essays in Nineteenth-Century Afro-American History.* Baton Rouge: Louisiana State University Press, 1986.

Blesser, Carol, ed. *In Joy and in Sorrow: Women, Family, and Marriage in the Victorian South, 1830–1900.* New York: Oxford University Press, 1991.

Block, Sharon. *Rape and Sexual Power in Early America.* Chapel Hill: University of North Carolina Press, 2006.

Brooks, Daphne. *Bodies in Dissent: Spectacular Performances of Race and Freedom, 1850–1910.* Durham, NC: Duke University Press, 2006.

Brooten, Bernadette J., ed., with Jacqueline L. Hazelton. *Beyond Slavery: Overcoming Its Religious and Sexual Legacies.* New York: Palgrave Macmillan, 2010.

Brown, Kathleen M. *Good Wives, Nasty Wenches, and Anxious Patriarchs: Gender, Race, and Power in Colonial Virginia.* Chapel Hill: University of North Carolina Press, 1996.

Butler, Judith. *Undoing Gender.* New York: Routledge, 2004.

Bynum, Victoria E. *Unruly Women: The Politics of Social and Sexual Control in the Old South.* Chapel Hill: University of North Carolina Press, 1992.

Calomiris, Charles W., and Jonathon B. Pritchett. "Preserving Slave Families for Profit: Traders' Incentives and Pricing in the New Orleans Slave Market." *Journal of Economic History* 69, no. 4 (2009): 986–1011.

Camp, Stephanie M. H. *Closer to Freedom: Enslaved Women and Everyday Resistance in the Plantation South.* Chapel Hill: University of North Carolina Press, 2004.

Caruth, Cathy. *Unclaimed Experience: Trauma, Narrative, and History.* Baltimore: Johns Hopkins University Press, 1996.

Clinton, Catherine, and Michele Gillespie, eds. *The Devil's Lane: Sex and Race in the Early South.* New York: Oxford University Press, 1997.

Collins, Patricia Hill. *Black Feminist Thought: Knowledge, Consciousness, and the Politics of Empowerment.* New York: Routledge, 1990.

Davis, Angela Y. *Women, Race, and Class.* New York: Vintage, 1983.

Digby, Anne. *Madness, Morality, and Medicine: A Study of the York Retreat, 1796–1914.* Cambridge: Cambridge University Press, 1985.

Dorsey, Jennifer Hull. *Hirelings: African American Workers and Free Labor in Early Maryland.* Ithaca, NY: Cornell University Press, 2011.

Dunaway, Wilma A. *The African-American Family in Slavery and Emancipation.* New York: Cambridge University Press, 2003.

Edwards, Laura F. "Enslaved Women and the Law: Paradoxes of Subordination in the Post-Revolutionary Carolinas." *Slavery and Abolition* 26, no. 2 (2005): 305–23.

———. "'The Marriage Covenant Is at the Foundation of All Our Rights': The Politics of Slave Marriages in North Carolina after Emancipation." *Law and History Review* 14, no. 1 (1996): 81–124.

Egerton, Douglas R. *Gabriel's Rebellion: The Virginia Slave Conspiracies of 1800 & 1802.* Chapel Hill: University of North Carolina Press, 1993.

Ellison, Mary. "Resistance to Oppression: Black Women's Response to Slavery in the United States." *Slavery and Abolition* 4, no. 1 (1983): 56–63.

Fields, Barbara Jeanne. *Slavery and Freedom on the Middle Ground: Maryland during the Nineteenth Century.* New Haven, CT: Yale University Press, 1985.

Finkelman, Paul. *An Imperfect Union: Slavery, Federalism, and Comity.* Chapel Hill: University of North Carolina Press, 1981.

———. "The Treason Trial of Castner Hanway." In *American Political Trials,* edited by Michal Belknap, 77–95. Westport, CT: Greenwood Press, 1994.

Fischer, Kirsten. *Suspect Relations: Sex, Race, and Resistance in Colonial North Carolina.* Ithaca, NY: Cornell University Press, 2002.

Fleischner, Jennifer. *Mastering Slavery: Memory, Family, and Identity in Women's Slaves Narratives.* New York: New York University Press, 1996.

Fox-Genovese, Elizabeth. *Within the Plantation Household: Black and White Women of the Old South.* Chapel Hill: University of North Carolina Press, 1988.

Franklin, John Hope, and Loren Schweninger. *Runaway Slaves: Rebels on the Plantation, 1790–1860.* New York: Oxford University Press, 1999.

Frederickson, Mary E., and Delores M. Walters, eds. *Gendered Resistance: Women, Slavery, and the Legacy of Margaret Garner.* Champaign: University of Illinois Press, 2013.

Freedman, Estelle B. *Redefining Rape: Sexual Violence in the Era of Suffrage and Segregation.* Cambridge, MA: Harvard University Press, 2013.

Gaspar, David Barry, and Darlene Clark Hine. *More Than Chattel: Black Women and Slavery in the Americas.* Bloomington: Indiana University Press, 1996.

Genovese, Eugene D. *Roll, Jordan, Roll: The World the Slaves Made.* New York: Vintage Books, 1974.

Glymph, Thavolia. *Out of the House of Bondage: The Transformation of the Plantation Household.* Cambridge: Cambridge University Press, 2008.

Gordon-Reed, Annette. *Thomas Jefferson and Sally Hemings: An American Controversy.* Charlottesville: University of Virginia Press, 1997.

———. *The Hemings of Monticello: An American Family.* New York: Norton, 2008.

Griffiths, Jennifer L. *Traumatic Possessions: The Body and Memory in African American Women's Writing and Performance.* Charlottesville: University of Virginia Press, 2010.

Gross, Ariela J. *Double Character: Slavery and Mastery in the Antebellum Southern Courtroom.* Athens: University of Georgia Press, 2006.

———. *What Blood Won't Tell: A History of Race on Trial in America.* Cambridge, MA: Harvard University Press, 2008.

———. "Litigating Whiteness: Trials of Racial Determination in the Nineteenth-Century South." *Yale Law Journal* 108, no. 1 (October 1998): 109–88.

Gutman, Herbert G. *The Black Family in Slavery and Freedom, 1750–1925.* New York: Vintage Books, 1977.

Hammonds, Evelynn M., and Rebecca M. Herzig. *The Nature of Difference: Sciences of Race in the United State from Jefferson to Genomics.* Cambridge, MA: MIT Press, 2009.

Harrison, Lowell Hayes. *A New History of Kentucky*. Lexington: University Press of Kentucky, 1997.

Hartman, Saidiya V. *Scenes of Subjection: Terror, Slavery, and Self-Making in Nineteenth-Century America*. New York: Oxford University Press, 1997.

Henderson, Carol E. *Scarring the Black Body: Race and Representation in African American Literature*. Columbia: University of Missouri Press, 2002.

Hine, Darlene Clark. *Hine Sight: Black Women and the Re-construction of American History*. Brooklyn: Carlson, 1994.

Hine, Darlene Clark, and Kate Wittenstein. "Female Slave Resistance: The Economics of Sex." In *The Black Woman Cross-Culturally*, edited by Filomina Chioma Steady, 289–99. Cambridge, MA: Schenkman, 1981.

Hodes, Martha. *White Women, Black Men: Illicit Sex in the 19th-Century South*. New Haven, CT: Yale University Press, 1997.

hooks, bell. "Healing Our Wounds: Liberatory Mental Health Care." In *Killing Rage: Ending Racism*, 133–45. New York: Henry Holt, 1995.

Horton, James Oliver, and Lois E. Horton. *In Hope of Liberty: Culture, Community and Protest among Northern Free Blacks, 1700–1860*. New York: Oxford University Press, 1997.

Howard, Victor B. *Black Liberation in Kentucky: Emancipation and Freedom, 1862–1884*. Lexington: University Press of Kentucky, 1983.

Jablonski, Nina G. *Living Color: The Biological and Social Meaning of Skin Color*. Berkeley: University of California Press, 2012.

Johnson, Walter. *Soul by Soul: Life inside the Antebellum Slave Market*. Cambridge, MA: Harvard University Press, 1999.

Jones, Anne Goodwyn, and Susan V. Donaldson, eds. *Haunted Bodies: Gender and Southern Texts*. Charlottesville: University Press of Virginia, 1997.

Jones, Bernie D. *Fathers of Conscience: Mixed-Race Inheritance in the Antebellum South*. Athens: University of Georgia Press, 2009.

———. "Southern Free Women of Color in the Antebellum North: Race, Class, and a 'New Women's Legal History.'" *Akron Law Review* 41, no. 3 (2008): 763–98.

Kaplan, Sara Clarke. "Love and Violence/Maternity and Death: Black Feminism and the Politics of Reading (Un)representability." *Black Women, Gender + Families* 1, no. 1 (Spring 2001): 94–124.

———. "Unspeakable Thoughts, Unthinkable Acts: Toward a Black Feminist Liberatory Politics." PhD diss., University of California, Berkeley, 2006.

Kilby, Jane. *Violence and the Cultural Politics of Trauma*. Edinburgh: Edinburgh University Press, 2007.

King, Debra Walker. *African Americans and the Culture of Pain*. Charlottesville: University of Virginia Press, 2008.

King, Wilma. "'Mad' Enough to Kill: Enslaved Women, Murder, and Southern Courts." *Journal of African American History* 92, no. 1, "Women, Slavery, and Historical Research" (Winter 2007): 37–56.

———. *Stolen Childhood: Slave Youth in Nineteenth-Century America*. Bloomington: Indiana University Press, 1995.

————. "The Mistress and Her Maids: White and Black Women in a Louisiana Household, 1858–1868." In *Discovering the Women in Slavery: Emancipating Perspectives on the American Past,* edited by Patricia Morton, 82–106. Athens: University of Georgia Press, 1996.

Kolchin, Peter. *American Slavery, 1619–1877.* New York: Hill and Wang, 1993.

LaCapra, Dominick. *Writing History, Writing Trauma.* Baltimore: Johns Hopkins University Press, 2013.

Lopez, Ian Hanley. *White by Law: The Legal Construction of Race.* New York: New York University Press, 2006.

Lucas, Marion Brunson. *A History of Blacks in Kentucky: From Slavery to Segregation, 1760–1891,* vol 1. Lexington: University Press of Kentucky, 2003.

Martin, Asa Earl. *The Anti-slavery Movement in Kentucky Prior to 1850.* Louisville: Standard Printing, 1918.

McLaurin, Melton A. *Celia, A Slave.* Athens: University of Georgia Press, 1991.

Middleton, Stephen. *Black Laws: Race and the Legal Process in Early Ohio.* Athens: Ohio University Press, 2005.

————. "The Fugitive Slave Crisis in Cincinnati, 1850–60." *Journal of Negro History* 72 (Winter–Spring 1987): 20–32.

Million, Joelle. *Woman's Voice, Woman's Place: Lucy Stone and the Birth of the Woman's Rights Movement.* Westport, CT: Praeger, 2003.

Mitchell, Sarah. "Mother, Murderess, or Martyr? Press Coverage of the Margaret Garner Story." In *Seeking a Voice: Images of Race and Gender in the 19th Century Press,* edited by David B. Sachsman, S. Kittrell Rushing, and Roy Morris Jr., 13–26. West Lafayette, IN: Purdue University Press, 2009.

Morrison, Toni. *Beloved: A Novel.* New York: Random House, 1987.

Muraskin, Roslyn., ed. *It's a Crime: Women and Justice.* New York: Prentice Hall, 2000.

Nudelman, Franny. "Harriet Jacobs and the Sentimental Politics of Female Suffering." *ELH* 59, no. 4 (Winter 1992): 939–64.

Painter, Nell Irvin. "Soul Murder and Slavery: Toward a Fully Loaded Cost Accounting." In *Southern History across the Color Line,* 15–39. Chapel Hill: University of North Carolina Press, 2002.

————. *Soul Murder and Slavery.* Waco, TX: Baylor University Press, 1995.

Rael, Patrick. *Eighty-Eight Years: The Long Death of Slavery in the United States, 1777–1865.* Athens: University of Georgia Press, 2015.

Reinhardt, Mark. *Who Speaks for Margaret Garner?* Minneapolis: University of Minnesota Press, 2010.

Roberts, Dorothy E. *Killing the Black Body: Race, Reproduction, and the Meaning of Liberty.* New York: Vintage Books, 1997.

————. "The Genetic Tie." *University of Chicago Law Review* 62, no. 1 (Winter 1995): 209–73.

————. "The Paradox of Silence and Display: Sexual Violation of Enslaved Women and Contemporary Contradictions in Black Female Sexuality." In *Beyond Slavery: Overcoming Its Religious and Sexual Legacies,* edited by Bernadette J. Brooten, 41–60. New York: Palgrave Macmillan, 2010.

Rothman, Joshua D. *Notorious in the Neighborhood: Sex and Families across the Color Line in Virginia, 1787–1861*. Chapel Hill: University of North Carolina Press, 2003.

Scarry, Elaine. *The Body in Pain: The Making and Unmaking of the World*. New York: Oxford University Press, 1985.

Scharff, Virginia. *The Women Jefferson Loved*. New York: Harper Perennial, 2010.

Schwartz, Marie Jenkins. *Birthing a Slave: Motherhood and Medicine in the Antebellum South*. Cambridge, MA: Harvard University Press, 2006.

———. *Born in Bondage: Growing Up Enslaved in the Antebellum South*. Cambridge, MA: Harvard University Press, 2000.

Showalter, Elaine. *The Female Malady: Women, Madness, and English Culture, 1830–1980*. New York: Penguin Books, 1987.

Smith, Merril D., ed. *Sex without Consent: Rape and Sexual Coercion in America*. New York: New York University Press, 2001.

Smithers, Gregory D. *Slave Breeding: Sex, Violence, and Memory in African American History*. Gainesville: University Press of Florida, 2012.

Snyder, Terri. *The Power to Die: Slavery and Suicide in British North America*. Chicago: University of Chicago Press, 2015.

Solinger, Rickie. *Pregnancy and Power: A Short History of Reproductive Politics in America*. New York: New York University Press, 2005.

Sommerville, Diane Miller. *Rape & Race in the Nineteenth-Century South*. Chapel Hill: University of North Carolina Press, 2004.

Spear, Jennifer M. *Race, Sex, and Social Order in Early New Orleans*. Baltimore: Johns Hopkins University Press, 2009.

Spillers, Hortense J. "Mama's Baby, Papa's Maybe: An American Grammar Book." In *African American Literary Theory: A Reader*, edited by Winston Napier, 257–79. New York: New York University Press, 2000.

Stevenson, Brenda. *Life in Black and White: Family and Community in the Slave South*. New York: Oxford University Press, 1996.

Sturm, Richard A., Neil F. Box, and Michele Ramsay. "Human Pigmentation Genetics: The Difference Is Only Skin Deep." *Bioessays* 20, no. 9 (1998): 712–21.

Sweet, Frank W. *Legal History of the Color Line: The Rise and Triumph of the One-Drop Rule*. Palm Coast, FL: Backintyme, 2005.

Tallant, Harold D. *Evil Necessity: Slavery and Political Culture in Antebellum Kentucky*. Lexington: University Press of Kentucky, 2003.

Taylor, Nikki M. *Frontiers of Freedom: Cincinnati's Black Community, 1802–1868*. Athens: Ohio University Press, 2005.

Tenney, Lauren J. "Psychiatric Slave No More: Parallels to a Black Liberation Psychology." *Radical Psychology* 7 (2008).

Warren, Wendy. "The Cause of Her Grief: The Rape of a Slave in Early New England." *Journal of American History* 93, no. 4 (2007): 1031–49.

Weisenburger, Steven. *Modern Medea: A Family Story of Slavery and Child-Murder from the Old South*. New York: Hill and Wang, 1998.

West, Emily. *Chains of Love: Slave Couples in Antebellum South Carolina*. Urbana: University of Illinois Press, 2004.

White, Deborah Gray. *Ar'n't I a Woman? Females Slaves in the Plantation South.* New York: W. W. Norton, 1985.

Williams, Heather Andrea. *Help Me to Find My People: The African American Search for Family Lost in Slavery.* Chapel Hill: University of North Carolina Press, 2012.

Wolff, Cynthia Griffin. "Margaret Garner: A Cincinnati Story." *Massachusetts Review* 32, no. 3 (Autumn 1991): 417–40.

Woolfork, Lisa. *Embodying American Slavery in Contemporary Culture.* Urbana: University of Illinois Press, 2009.

Wyatt-Brown, Bertram. *Southern Honor: Ethics & Behavior in the Old South.* New York: Oxford University Press, 2007.

Yanuck, Julius. "The Garner Fugitive Slave Case." *Mississippi Valley Historical Review* 40, no. 2 (June 1953): 47–66.

Yarbrough, Fay A. "Power, Perception, and Interracial Sex: Former Slaves Recall a Multiracial South." *Journal of Southern History* 17, no. 3 (August 2005): 559–88.

Zaborney, John J. *Slaves for Hire: Renting Enslaved Laborers in Antebellum Virginia.* Baton Rouge: Louisiana State University Press, 2012.

INDEX

CPSIA information can be obtained
at www.ICGtesting.com
Printed in the USA
FFOW02n0834250317
33689FF